PRESENTED TO

FROM

DATE

God's Answers® for the GRAADUATE

CLASS OF 2020

Compiled by Jack Countryman

An Imprint of Thomas Nelson Publishers

THOMAS NELSON
Since 1798

God's Answers® for the Graduate: Class of 2020
© 2020 by Jack Countryman

Published in Nashville, Tennessee, by Thomas Nelson. Thomas Nelson is a registered trademark of HarperCollins Christian Publishing, Inc.

Scripture quotations are taken from the New King James Version®. © 1982 by Thomas Nelson. Used by permission. All rights reserved.

Thomas Nelson titles may be purchased in bulk for educational, business, fund-raising, or sales promotional use. For information, please e-mail SpecialMarkets@ ThomasNelson.com.

ISBN: 978-1-4002-1554-6
ISBN: 978-1-4041-1289-6 (Custom)

Printed in China

20 21 22 23 24 DSC 5 4 3 2 1

Contents

Foreword

God has all the answers to life, and they are found in His Word. We created this book to help the graduate stay close to the foundation of the Christian walk through easy-to-read topical subjects.

As you seek a higher education or go out into the job market, there will be many distractions that seem appealing but can lead you away from your goals and from Christ. Sometimes your own ambition and desire for success will steer you away from God's plans for you and lead you into destruction and chaos. Our eldest son, Bret, got caught in that trap and had to work through many challenges before he found his way back to what God had planned for him. We are happy to say he is now using those experiences to help others, all to the glory of God.

Our hope is that you will use this book to open your eyes and see what God has planned for you. The various topics, such as "How Can I Handle Disappointment?", "How Can the Choices I Make Determine the Lifestyle I Live?", and many others, will benefit you in your daily walk with Him.

May you find joy, peace, and contentment as you seek God's answers in this book.

Jack and Marsha Countryman

Dear Graduate,

Growing up in a solid Christian family has given me a firm foundation on which to stand. But when I left home after graduation, I took the fast track of life and started running with the wrong crowd. I did this for quite a while and, as time went on, I became worn down mentally, physically, spiritually, and emotionally. During that tumultuous time, I lost someone very near and dear to me. I believe I lost even myself. At times, fear and anxiety gripped my life, and I thought there would be no tomorrow. I allowed others to lead me down a very destructive road.

It took many years of strife before I turned back to God. However, I know that all along, God's love for me never wavered. He patiently waited for me to wake up and grow up. Fortunately, I did.

Now I spend my time celebrating how He's redeemed the time I lost and truly appreciating the fact that without Jesus Christ at the helm of my life, I would be nothing.

As you read the Scriptures in this book, may your journey be forever changed. And may you always know this: God is waiting for you. He has big plans for you. Realizing this and really knowing your identity in Christ is a very mature thing to do.

Congratulations on your graduation. May you always seek Him and His ways for your life.

Bret Countryman

God's
Answers
for Me . . .

God's Answers *for* Me . . .

WHO IS GOD?

—⟡————————————⟡—

"I am the Alpha and the Omega, the Beginning and the End," says the Lord, "who is and who was and who is to come, the Almighty."

REVELATION 1:8

The LORD by wisdom founded the earth;
    By understanding He established the heavens;
By His knowledge the depths were broken up,
    And clouds drop down the dew.
My son, let them not depart from your eyes—
    Keep sound wisdom and discretion;
So they will be life to your soul
    And grace to your neck.
Then you will walk safely in your way,
    And your foot will not stumble.

PROVERBS 3:19–23

Hear, O Israel: The LORD our God, the LORD is one!

DEUTERONOMY 6:4

For the ways of man are before the eyes of
      the LORD,
  And He ponders all his paths.

PROVERBS 5:21

In the beginning God created the heavens and the earth. The earth was without form, and void; and darkness was on the face of the deep. And the Spirit of God was hovering over the face of the waters.

Then God said, "Let there be light"; and there was light. And God saw the light, that it was good; and God divided the light from the darkness. God called the light Day, and the darkness He called Night. So the evening and the morning were the first day.

GENESIS 1:1–5

Then God said, "Let Us make man in Our image, according to Our likeness; let them have dominion over the fish of the sea, over the birds of the air, and over the cattle, over all the earth and over every creeping thing that creeps on the earth." So God created man in His own image; in the image of God He created him; male and female He created them.

GENESIS 1:26–27

And the LORD God formed man of the dust of the ground, and breathed into his nostrils the breath of life; and man became a living being.

GENESIS 2:7

Commit your works to the LORD,
    And your thoughts will be established.
The LORD has made all for Himself,
    Yes, even the wicked for the day of doom.

PROVERBS 16:3–4

The eyes of the LORD are in every place,
    Keeping watch on the evil and the good.

PROVERBS 15:3

God's Answers *for* Me . . .

WHERE DO I SEEK TRUTH?

⚜———————————⚜

Let not mercy and truth forsake you;
    Bind them around your neck,
    Write them on the tablet of your heart,
And so find favor and high esteem
    In the sight of God and man.

PROVERBS 3:3–4

Incline your ear and hear the words of the wise,
    And apply your heart to my knowledge;
For it is a pleasant thing if you keep them
            within you;
    Let them all be fixed upon your lips.

PROVERBS 22:17–18

Show me Your ways, O LORD;
    Teach me Your paths.
Lead me in Your truth and teach me,
    For You are the God of my salvation;
    On You I wait all the day.

PSALM 25:4–5

He shall cover you with His feathers,
And under His wings you shall take refuge;
His truth shall be your shield and buckler.

PSALM 91:4

Praise the LORD, all you Gentiles!
Laud Him, all you peoples!
For His merciful kindness is great toward us,
And the truth of the LORD endures forever.

PSALM 117:1–2

Serve the LORD with gladness;
Come before His presence with singing.
Know that the LORD, He is God;
It is He who has made us, and not we ourselves;
We are His people and the sheep of His pasture.
Enter into His gates with thanksgiving,
And into His courts with praise.
Be thankful to Him, and bless His name.
For the LORD is good;
His mercy is everlasting,
And His truth endures to all generations.

PSALM 100:2–5

Jesus said to him, "I am the way, the truth, and the life. No one comes to the Father except through Me."

JOHN 14:6

Then Jesus said to those Jews who believed Him, "If you abide in My word, you are My disciples indeed. And you shall know the truth, and the truth shall make you free."

JOHN 8:31–32

God's Answers *for* Me . . .

HOW CAN I MAKE SELF-CONTROL KEY IN MY LIFE?

❦━━━━━━━━━━━━━━━━━❦

Keep your heart with all diligence,
    For out of it spring the issues of life.
Put away from you a deceitful mouth,
    And put perverse lips far from you.
Let your eyes look straight ahead,
    And your eyelids look right before you.
Ponder the path of your feet,
    And let all your ways be established.
Do not turn to the right or the left;
    Remove your foot from evil.

PROVERBS 4:23–27

For a bishop must be . . . hospitable, a lover of what is good, sober-minded, just, holy, self-controlled, holding fast the faithful word as he has been taught, that he may be able, by sound doctrine, both to exhort and convict those who contradict.

TITUS 1:7–9

In this you greatly rejoice, though now for a little while, if need be, you have been grieved by various trials, that the genuineness of your faith, being much more precious than gold that perishes, though it is tested by fire, may be found to praise, honor, and glory at the revelation of Jesus Christ, whom having not seen you love. Though now you do not see Him, yet believing, you rejoice with joy inexpressible and full of glory.

1 PETER 1:6–8

Whoever has no rule over his own spirit
Is like a city broken down, without walls.

PROVERBS 25:28

Do you not know that those who run in a race all run, but one receives the prize? Run in such a way that you may obtain it. And everyone who competes for the prize is temperate in all things. Now they do it to obtain a perishable crown, but we for an imperishable crown. Therefore I run thus: not with uncertainty. Thus I fight: not as one who beats the air. But I discipline my body and bring it into subjection, lest, when I have preached to others, I myself should become disqualified.

1 CORINTHIANS 9:24–27

He who is slow to anger is better than the
      mighty,
  And he who rules his spirit than he who
      takes a city.

PROVERBS 16:32

But the fruit of the Spirit is love, joy, peace, long-suffering, kindness, goodness, faithfulness, gentleness, self-control. Against such there is no law.

GALATIANS 5:22–23

God's Answers *for* Me . . .

HOW DO I LET GOD
DIRECT MY PATH?

❧————————————————☙

When a man's ways please the LORD,
 He makes even his enemies to be at peace
  with him.
Better is a little with righteousness,
 Than vast revenues without justice.
A man's heart plans his way,
 But the LORD directs his steps.

PROVERBS 16:7–9

All the ways of a man are pure in his own eyes,
 But the LORD weighs the spirits.
Commit your works to the LORD,
 And your thoughts will be established.

PROVERBS 16:2–3

A man's steps are of the LORD;
 How then can a man understand his
  own way?

PROVERBS 20:24

Listen to counsel and receive instruction,
    That you may be wise in your latter days.
There are many plans in a man's heart,
    Nevertheless the LORD's counsel—that
        will stand.

PROVERBS 19:20–21

My son, keep your father's command,
    And do not forsake the law of your mother.
Bind them continually upon your heart;
    Tie them around your neck.
When you roam, they will lead you;
    When you sleep, they will keep you;
    And when you awake, they will speak
        with you.
For the commandment is a lamp,
    And the law a light;
    Reproofs of instruction are the way of life.

PROVERBS 6:20–23

My son, do not forget my law,
    But let your heart keep my commands;
For length of days and long life
    And peace they will add to you.

PROVERBS 3:1–2

Hear, my children, the instruction of a father,
And give attention to know understanding;
For I give you good doctrine:
Do not forsake my law.
When I was my father's son,
Tender and the only one in the sight of
my mother,
He also taught me, and said to me:
"Let your heart retain my words;
Keep my commands, and live."

PROVERBS 4:1–4

Hear, my son, and receive my sayings,
And the years of your life will be many.
I have taught you in the way of wisdom;
I have led you in right paths.
When you walk, your steps will not be hindered,
And when you run, you will not stumble.
Take firm hold of instruction, do not let go;
Keep her, for she is your life.

PROVERBS 4:10–13

God's Answers *for* Me . . .

How Can I Live My Dreams?

❦————————————————❧

The king shall have joy in Your strength,
     O Lord;
   And in Your salvation how greatly
      shall he rejoice!
You have given him his heart's desire,
   And have not withheld the request of his lips.
For You meet him with the blessings of goodness;
   You set a crown of pure gold upon his head.
He asked life from You, and You gave it
     to him—
   Length of days forever and ever.
His glory is great in Your salvation;
   Honor and majesty You have placed upon him.
For You have made him most blessed forever;
   You have made him exceedingly glad
     with Your presence.
For the king trusts in the Lord,
   And through the mercy of the Most High he
     shall not be moved.

PSALM 21:1–7

Happy is the man who finds wisdom,
  And the man who gains understanding;
For her proceeds are better than the profits
      of silver,
  And her gain than fine gold.
She is more precious than rubies,
  And all the things you may desire cannot
      compare with her.
Length of days is in her right hand,
  In her left hand riches and honor.
Her ways are ways of pleasantness,
  And all her paths are peace.
She is a tree of life to those who take hold of her,
  And happy are all who retain her.

PROVERBS 3:13–18

Do not be rash with your mouth,
  And let not your heart utter anything hastily
      before God.
  For God is in heaven, and you on earth;
  Therefore let your words be few.
For a dream comes through much activity,
  And a fool's voice is known by his
      many words.

ECCLESIASTES 5:2–3

Now the LORD had said to Abram: . . .
"I will make you a great nation;
I will bless you
And make your name great;
And you shall be a blessing.
I will bless those who bless you,
And I will curse him who curses you;
And in you all the families of the earth
shall be blessed."
So Abram departed as the LORD had spoken to him, and Lot went with him. And Abram was seventy-five years old when he departed from Haran.

GENESIS 12:1–4

"And it shall come to pass afterward
That I will pour out My Spirit on all flesh;
Your sons and your daughters shall prophesy,
Your old men shall dream dreams,
Your young men shall see visions.
And also on My menservants and on My
maidservants
I will pour out My Spirit in those days.
And I will show wonders in the heavens
and in the earth."

JOEL 2:28–30

Trust in the LORD, and do good;
   Dwell in the land, and feed on His faithfulness.
Delight yourself also in the LORD,
   And He shall give you the desires of
         your heart.
Commit your way to the LORD,
   Trust also in Him,
   And He shall bring it to pass.
He shall bring forth your righteousness as
         the light,
   And your justice as the noonday.

PSALM 37:3–6

God's Answers *for* Me . . .

HOW CAN THE CHOICES I MAKE DETERMINE THE LIFESTYLE I LIVE?

❧————————————❧

I say then: Walk in the Spirit, and you shall not fulfill the lust of the flesh. For the flesh lusts against the Spirit, and the Spirit against the flesh; and these are contrary to one another, so that you do not do the things that you wish.

GALATIANS 5:16–17

Do not be deceived, God is not mocked; for whatever a man sows, that he will also reap. For he who sows to his flesh will of the flesh reap corruption, but he who sows to the Spirit will of the Spirit reap everlasting life. And let us not grow weary while doing good, for in due season we shall reap if we do not lose heart. Therefore, as we have opportunity, let us do good to all, especially to those who are of the household of faith.

GALATIANS 6:7–10

Therefore lay aside all filthiness and overflow of wickedness, and receive with meekness the implanted word, which is able to save your souls.

But be doers of the word, and not hearers only, deceiving yourselves. For if anyone is a hearer of the word and not a doer, he is like a man observing his natural face in a mirror; for he observes himself, goes away, and immediately forgets what kind of man he was. But he who looks into the perfect law of liberty and continues in it, and is not a forgetful hearer but a doer of the work, this one will be blessed in what he does.

JAMES 1:21–25

I have been crucified with Christ; it is no longer I who live, but Christ lives in me; and the life which I now live in the flesh I live by faith in the Son of God, who loved me and gave Himself for me.

GALATIANS 2:20

Who is wise and understanding among you? Let him show by good conduct that his works are done in the meekness of wisdom.

JAMES 3:13

Then He said to His disciples, "Therefore I say to you, do not worry about your life, what you will eat; nor about the body, what you will put on. Life is more than food, and the body is more than clothing. Consider the ravens, for they neither sow nor reap, which have neither storehouse nor barn; and God feeds them. Of how much more value are you than the birds? And which of you by worrying can add one cubit to his stature? If you then are not able to do the least, why are you anxious for the rest? Consider the lilies, how they grow: they neither toil nor spin; and yet I say to you, even Solomon in all his glory was not arrayed like one of these. If then God so clothes the grass, which today is in the field and tomorrow is thrown into the oven, how much more will He clothe you, O you of little faith?

"And do not seek what you should eat or what you should drink, nor have an anxious mind. For all these things the nations of the world seek after, and your Father knows that you need these things. But seek the kingdom of God, and all these things shall be added to you."

LUKE 12:22–31

God's Answers *for* Me . . .

HOW IS THE WAY OF THE LORD MY STRENGTH?

❧━━━━━━━━━━━━━━━━❧

The name of the LORD is a strong tower;
    The righteous run to it and are safe.

PROVERBS 18:10

Be of good courage,
    And He shall strengthen your heart,
    All you who hope in the LORD.

PSALM 31:24

In the fear of the LORD there is strong
        confidence,
    And His children will have a place of refuge.

PROVERBS 14:26

A wise man is strong,
    Yes, a man of knowledge increases strength;
For by wise counsel you will wage your own war,
    And in a multitude of counselors there is safety.

PROVERBS 24:5–6

The LORD by wisdom founded the earth;
    By understanding He established the heavens;
By His knowledge the depths were broken up,
    And clouds drop down the dew.
My son, let them not depart from your eyes—
    Keep sound wisdom and discretion;
So they will be life to your soul
    And grace to your neck.
Then you will walk safely in your way,
    And your foot will not stumble.
When you lie down, you will not be afraid;
    Yes, you will lie down and your sleep
        will be sweet.
Do not be afraid of sudden terror,
    Nor of trouble from the wicked when it comes;
For the LORD will be your confidence,
    And will keep your foot from being caught.

PROVERBS 3:19–26

And they kept the Feast of Unleavened Bread
seven days with joy; for the LORD made them joy-
ful, and turned the heart of the king of Assyria
toward them, to strengthen their hands in the
work of the house of God, the God of Israel.

EZRA 6:22

God's Answers *for* Me . . .

WHAT ARE THE PERILS OF LIVING WITH THE DEVIL?

So when the woman saw that the tree was good for food, that it was pleasant to the eyes, and a tree desirable to make one wise, she took of its fruit and ate. She also gave to her husband with her, and he ate. Then the eyes of both of them were opened, and they knew that they were naked; and they sewed fig leaves together and made themselves coverings.

And they heard the sound of the LORD God walking in the garden in the cool of the day, and Adam and his wife hid themselves from the presence of the LORD God among the trees of the garden.

Then the LORD God called to Adam and said to him, "Where are you?"

So he said, "I heard Your voice in the garden, and I was afraid because I was naked; and I hid myself."

GENESIS 3:6–10

"Why do you not understand My speech? Because you are not able to listen to My word. You are of your father the devil, and the desires of your father you want to do. He was a murderer from the beginning, and does not stand in the truth, because there is no truth in him. When he speaks a lie, he speaks from his own resources, for he is a liar and the father of it. But because I tell the truth, you do not believe Me. Which of you convicts Me of sin? And if I tell the truth, why do you not believe Me? He who is of God hears God's words; therefore you do not hear, because you are not of God."

JOHN 8:43–47

"The lamp of the body is the eye. Therefore, when your eye is good, your whole body also is full of light. But when your eye is bad, your body also is full of darkness."

LUKE 11:34

Therefore submit to God. Resist the devil and he will flee from you. Draw near to God and He will draw near to you. Cleanse your hands, you sinners; and purify your hearts, you double-minded.

JAMES 4:7–8

Be sober, be vigilant; because your adversary the devil walks about like a roaring lion, seeking whom he may devour. Resist him, steadfast in the faith, knowing that the same sufferings are experienced by your brotherhood in the world. But may the God of all grace, who called us to His eternal glory by Christ Jesus, after you have suffered a while, perfect, establish, strengthen, and settle you. To Him be the glory and the dominion forever and ever. Amen.

1 PETER 5:8–11

"The thief does not come except to steal, and to kill, and to destroy. I have come that they may have life, and that they may have it more abundantly.

"I am the good shepherd. The good shepherd gives His life for the sheep."

JOHN 10:10–11

"Who walks in darkness
And has no light?
Let him trust in the name of the LORD
And rely upon his God."

ISAIAH 50:10

Little children, let no one deceive you. He who practices righteousness is righteous, just as He is righteous. He who sins is of the devil, for the devil has sinned from the beginning. For this purpose the Son of God was manifested, that He might destroy the works of the devil. Whoever has been born of God does not sin, for His seed remains in him; and he cannot sin, because he has been born of God.

1 JOHN 3:7–9

Put on the whole armor of God, that you may be able to stand against the wiles of the devil. For we do not wrestle against flesh and blood, but against principalities, against powers, against the rulers of the darkness of this age, against spiritual hosts of wickedness in the heavenly places. Therefore take up the whole armor of God, that you may be able to withstand in the evil day, and having done all, to stand.

EPHESIANS 6:11–13

God's Answers *for* Me . . .

HOW DOES GOD HONOR THE HUMBLE?

❧―――――――――❧

The fear of the LORD is the instruction of wisdom,
  And before honor is humility.

PROVERBS 15:33

Before destruction the heart of a man is haughty,
  And before honor is humility.

PROVERBS 18:12

By humility and the fear of the LORD
  Are riches and honor and life.

PROVERBS 22:4

A man's pride will bring him low,
  But the humble in spirit will retain honor.

PROVERBS 29:23

When pride comes, then comes shame;
  But with the humble is wisdom.

PROVERBS 11:2

The LORD lifts up the humble;
     He casts the wicked down to the ground.
                                        PSALM 147:6

LORD, You have heard the desire of the humble;
     You will prepare their heart;
     You will cause Your ear to hear,
To do justice to the fatherless and the oppressed,
     That the man of the earth may oppress
          no more.
                                        PSALM 10:17–18

For thus says the High and Lofty One
     Who inhabits eternity, whose name is Holy:
     "I dwell in the high and holy place,
     With him who has a contrite and
          humble spirit,
     To revive the spirit of the humble,
     And to revive the heart of the contrite ones."
                                        ISAIAH 57:15

God's Answers *for* Me . . .

WHY WAIT UNTIL AFTER MARRIAGE TO HAVE SEXUAL RELATIONS?

———————————

Let your fountain be blessed,
  And rejoice with the wife of your youth.
As a loving deer and a graceful doe,
  Let her breasts satisfy you at all times;
  And always be enraptured with her love.
For why should you, my son, be enraptured
        by an immoral woman,
  And be embraced in the arms of a seductress?
For the ways of man are before the eyes of
        the LORD,
  And He ponders all his paths.

PROVERBS 5:18–21

He who loves purity of heart
  And has grace on his lips,
  The king will be his friend.

PROVERBS 22:11

Flee sexual immorality. Every sin that a man does is outside the body, but he who commits sexual immorality sins against his own body. Or do you not know that your body is the temple of the Holy Spirit who is in you, whom you have from God, and you are not your own? For you were bought at a price; therefore glorify God in your body and in your spirit, which are God's.

1 Corinthians 6:18–20

For this is the will of God, your sanctification: that you should abstain from sexual immorality; that each of you should know how to possess his own vessel in sanctification and honor, not in passion of lust, like the Gentiles who do not know God; that no one should take advantage of and defraud his brother in this matter, because the Lord is the avenger of all such, as we also forewarned you and testified. For God did not call us to uncleanness, but in holiness.

1 Thessalonians 4:3–7

Let no one despise your youth, but be an example to the believers in word, in conduct, in love, in spirit, in faith, in purity.

1 Timothy 4:12

God's Answers *for* Me . . .

WHAT IS INAPPROPRIATE SEXUAL BEHAVIOR?

❧———————————❧

Let us walk properly, as in the day, not in revelry and drunkenness, not in lewdness and lust, not in strife and envy. But put on the Lord Jesus Christ, and make no provision for the flesh, to fulfill its lusts.

ROMANS 13:13–14

"You have heard that it was said to those of old, 'You shall not commit adultery.' But I say to you that whoever looks at a woman to lust for her has already committed adultery with her in his heart."

MATTHEW 5:27–28

Marriage is honorable among all, and the bed undefiled; but fornicators and adulterers God will judge.

HEBREWS 13:4

I say then: Walk in the Spirit, and you shall not fulfill the lust of the flesh. For the flesh lusts against the Spirit, and the Spirit against the flesh; and these are contrary to one another, so that you do not do the things that you wish.

GALATIANS 5:16–17

Professing to be wise, they became fools, and changed the glory of the incorruptible God into an image made like corruptible man. . . .

For this reason God gave them up to vile passions. For even their women exchanged the natural use for what is against nature. Likewise also the men, leaving the natural use of the woman, burned in their lust for one another, men with men committing what is shameful, and receiving in themselves the penalty of their error which was due.

And even as they did not like to retain God in their knowledge, God gave them over to a debased mind, to do those things which are not fitting; being filled with all unrighteousness, [and] sexual immorality.

ROMANS 1:22–23, 26–29

For the commandment is a lamp,
    And the law a light;
    Reproofs of instruction are the way of life,
To keep you from the evil woman,
    From the flattering tongue of a seductress.
Do not lust after her beauty in your heart,
    Nor let her allure you with her eyelids.
For by means of a harlot
    A man is reduced to a crust of bread;
    And an adulteress will prey upon his
        precious life.
Can a man take fire to his bosom,
    And his clothes not be burned?
Can one walk on hot coals,
    And his feet not be seared?
So is he who goes in to his neighbor's wife;
    Whoever touches her shall not be innocent. . . .
Whoever commits adultery with a woman lacks
        understanding;
    He who does so destroys his own soul.

PROVERBS 6:23–29, 32

God's Answers *for* Me . . .

WHAT DOES GOD SAY ABOUT SUBSTANCE ABUSE?

For the grace of God that brings salvation has appeared to all men, teaching us that, denying ungodliness and worldly lusts, we should live soberly, righteously, and godly in the present age.

TITUS 2:11–12

But let us who are of the day be sober, putting on the breastplate of faith and love, and as a helmet the hope of salvation.

1 THESSALONIANS 5:8

The night is far spent, the day is at hand. Therefore let us cast off the works of darkness, and let us put on the armor of light. Let us walk properly, as in the day, not in revelry and drunkenness, not in lewdness and lust, not in strife and envy. But put on the Lord Jesus Christ, and make no provision for the flesh, to fulfill its lusts.

ROMANS 13:12–14

See then that you walk circumspectly, not as fools but as wise, redeeming the time, because the days are evil.

Therefore do not be unwise, but understand what the will of the Lord is. And do not be drunk with wine, in which is dissipation; but be filled with the Spirit.

EPHESIANS 5:15–18

Or do you not know that your body is the temple of the Holy Spirit who is in you, whom you have from God, and you are not your own? For you were bought at a price; therefore glorify God in your body and in your spirit, which are God's.

1 CORINTHIANS 6:19–20

God's Answers *for* Me . . .

WHAT DO I DO WHEN NOTHING IS GOING RIGHT?

Wait on the LORD;
  Be of good courage,
  And He shall strengthen your heart;
  Wait, I say, on the LORD!

PSALM 27:14

My brethren, count it all joy when you fall into various trials, knowing that the testing of your faith produces patience. But let patience have its perfect work, that you may be perfect and complete, lacking nothing. If any of you lacks wisdom, let him ask of God, who gives to all liberally and without reproach, and it will be given to him. But let him ask in faith, with no doubting, for he who doubts is like a wave of the sea driven and tossed by the wind. For let not that man suppose that he will receive anything from the Lord; he is a double-minded man, unstable in all his ways.

JAMES 1:2–8

But those who wait on the LORD
    Shall renew their strength;
    They shall mount up with wings like eagles,
    They shall run and not be weary,
    They shall walk and not faint.

ISAIAH 40:31

Hear my cry, O God;
    Attend to my prayer.
From the end of the earth I will cry to You,
    When my heart is overwhelmed;
    Lead me to the rock that is higher than I.
For You have been a shelter for me,
    A strong tower from the enemy.

PSALM 61:1–3

If we confess our sins, He is faithful and just to forgive us our sins and to cleanse us from all unrighteousness.

1 JOHN 1:9

Pray without ceasing, in everything give thanks; for this is the will of God in Christ Jesus for you.

1 THESSALONIANS 5:17–18

Let us draw near with a true heart in full assurance of faith, having our hearts sprinkled from an evil conscience and our bodies washed with pure water. Let us hold fast the confession of our hope without wavering, for He who promised is faithful. And let us consider one another in order to stir up love and good works.

HEBREWS 10:22–24

God's Answers *for* Me . . .

WHAT IS THE GIFT OF FORGIVENESS?

In Him we have redemption through His blood, the forgiveness of sins, according to the riches of His grace which He made to abound toward us in all wisdom and prudence.

EPHESIANS 1:7–8

For as the heavens are high above the earth,
    So great is His mercy toward those who
        fear Him;
As far as the east is from the west,
    So far has He removed our transgressions
        from us.

PSALM 103:11–12

Therefore, if anyone is in Christ, he is a new creation; old things have passed away; behold, all things have become new.

2 CORINTHIANS 5:17

LORD, You have been favorable to Your land;
    You have brought back the captivity of Jacob.
You have forgiven the iniquity of Your people;
    You have covered all their sin.
You have taken away all Your wrath;
    You have turned from the fierceness of
        Your anger.

PSALM 85:1–3

"Come now, and let us reason together,"
    Says the LORD,
    "Though your sins are like scarlet,
    They shall be as white as snow;
    Though they are red like crimson,
    They shall be as wool."

ISAIAH 1:18

The God of our fathers raised up Jesus whom
you murdered by hanging on a tree. Him God
has exalted to His right hand to be Prince and
Savior, to give repentance to Israel and forgiveness of sins. And we are His witnesses to these
things, and so also is the Holy Spirit whom God
has given to those who obey Him.

ACTS 5:30–32

"I, even I, am He who blots out your
          transgressions for My own sake;
     And I will not remember your sins.
Put Me in remembrance;
     Let us contend together;
     State your case, that you may be acquitted."
                                        ISAIAH 43:25–26

Blessed is he whose transgression is forgiven,
     Whose sin is covered.
Blessed is the man to whom the LORD does
          not impute iniquity,
     And in whose spirit there is no deceit.
                                        PSALM 32:1–2

Blessed are those whose lawless deeds are forgiven, and whose sins are covered.
                                        ROMANS 4:7

God's Answers *for* Me . . .

HOW IS FRIENDSHIP A BLESSING?

A man who has friends must himself be friendly,
But there is a friend who sticks closer than
a brother.

PROVERBS 18:24

Ointment and perfume delight the heart,
And the sweetness of a man's friend gives
delight by hearty counsel.

PROVERBS 27:9

Do you not know that friendship with the world
is enmity with God? Whoever therefore wants to
be a friend of the world makes himself an enemy
of God.

JAMES 4:4

As iron sharpens iron,
So a man sharpens the countenance of
his friend.

PROVERBS 27:17

Do not forsake your own friend or your
       father's friend,
   Nor go to your brother's house in the day
       of your calamity;
   Better is a neighbor nearby than a brother
       far away.

PROVERBS 27:10

Two are better than one,
   Because they have a good reward for
       their labor.

ECCLESIASTES 4:9

"No longer do I call you servants, for a servant does not know what his master is doing; but I have called you friends, for all things that I heard from My Father I have made known to you."

JOHN 15:15

And the Scripture was fulfilled which says, "Abraham believed God, and it was accounted to him for righteousness." And he was called the friend of God.

JAMES 2:23

God's Answers *for* Me . . .

WHAT ARE THE REASONS FOR OBEDIENCE?

⇛————————————⇝

My son, hear the instruction of your father,
   And do not forsake the law of your mother;
For they will be a graceful ornament on
      your head,
   And chains about your neck.

PROVERBS 1:8–9

Therefore gird up the loins of your mind, be sober, and rest your hope fully upon the grace that is to be brought to you at the revelation of Jesus Christ; as obedient children, not conforming yourselves to the former lusts, as in your ignorance; but as He who called you is holy, you also be holy in all your conduct, because it is written, "Be holy, for I am holy."

1 PETER 1:13–16

"But why do you call Me 'Lord, Lord,' and not do the things which I say? Whoever comes to Me, and hears My sayings and does them, I will show you whom he is like: He is like a man building a house, who dug deep and laid the foundation on the rock. And when the flood arose, the stream beat vehemently against that house, and could not shake it, for it was founded on the rock. But he who heard and did nothing is like a man who built a house on the earth without a foundation, against which the stream beat vehemently; and immediately it fell. And the ruin of that house was great."

LUKE 6:46–49

Children, obey your parents in the Lord, for this is right. "Honor your father and mother," which is the first commandment with promise: "that it may be well with you and you may live long on the earth."

EPHESIANS 6:1–3

For if in anything I have boasted to him about you, I am not ashamed. But as we spoke all things to you in truth, even so our boasting to Titus was found true. And his affections are greater for you as he remembers the obedience of you all, how with fear and trembling you received him. Therefore I rejoice that I have confidence in you in everything.

2 Corinthians 7:14–16

For the administration of this service not only supplies the needs of the saints, but also is abounding through many thanksgivings to God, while, through the proof of this ministry, they glorify God for the obedience of your confession to the gospel of Christ, and for your liberal sharing with them and all men, and by their prayer for you, who long for you because of the exceeding grace of God in you. Thanks be to God for His indescribable gift!

2 Corinthians 9:12–15

For as by one man's disobedience many were made sinners, so also by one Man's obedience many will be made righteous.

Romans 5:19

And being found in appearance as a man, He humbled Himself and became obedient to the point of death, even the death of the cross. Therefore God also has highly exalted Him and given Him the name which is above every name, that at the name of Jesus every knee should bow, of those in heaven, and of those on earth, and of those under the earth, and that every tongue should confess that Jesus Christ is Lord, to the glory of God the Father.

PHILIPPIANS 2:8–11

Do not love the world or the things in the world. If anyone loves the world, the love of the Father is not in him. For all that is in the world—the lust of the flesh, the lust of the eyes, and the pride of life—is not of the Father but is of the world. And the world is passing away, and the lust of it; but he who does the will of God abides forever.

1 JOHN 2:15–17

God's Answers *for* Me . . .

HOW DOES HAVING HONORABLE CHARACTER INFLUENCE MY LIFE?

———————⚜———————

"I am the true vine, and My Father is the vine-dresser. Every branch in Me that does not bear fruit He takes away; and every branch that bears fruit He prunes, that it may bear more fruit."

JOHN 15:1–2

Therefore, having been justified by faith, we have peace with God through our Lord Jesus Christ, through whom also we have access by faith into this grace in which we stand, and rejoice in hope of the glory of God. And not only that, but we also glory in tribulations, knowing that tribulation produces perseverance; and perseverance, character; and character, hope. Now hope does not disappoint, because the love of God has been poured out in our hearts by the Holy Spirit who was given to us.

ROMANS 5:1–5

Therefore, as the elect of God, holy and beloved, put on tender mercies, kindness, humility, meekness, longsuffering; bearing with one another, and forgiving one another, if anyone has a complaint against another; even as Christ forgave you, so you also must do. But above all these things put on love, which is the bond of perfection. And let the peace of God rule in your hearts, to which also you were called in one body; and be thankful. Let the word of Christ dwell in you richly in all wisdom, teaching and admonishing one another in psalms and hymns and spiritual songs, singing with grace in your hearts to the Lord. And whatever you do in word or deed, do all in the name of the Lord Jesus, giving thanks to God the Father through Him.

COLOSSIANS 3:12–17

But also for this very reason, giving all diligence, add to your faith virtue, to virtue knowledge, to knowledge self-control, to self-control perseverance, to perseverance godliness, to godliness brotherly kindness, and to brotherly kindness love.

2 PETER 1:5–7

Now godliness with contentment is great gain. For we brought nothing into this world, and it is certain we can carry nothing out. And having food and clothing, with these we shall be content. But those who desire to be rich fall into temptation and a snare, and into many foolish and harmful lusts which drown men in destruction and perdition.

1 TIMOTHY 6:6–9

Grace and peace be multiplied to you in the knowledge of God and of Jesus our Lord, as His divine power has given to us all things that pertain to life and godliness, through the knowledge of Him who called us by glory and virtue, by which have been given to us exceedingly great and precious promises, that through these you may be partakers of the divine nature, having escaped the corruption that is in the world through lust.

2 PETER 1:2–4

God's Answers *for* Me . . .

HOW CAN I BUILD MY SELF-CONFIDENCE?

⇠————————————⇢

O God, You are more awesome than Your
       holy places.
   The God of Israel is He who gives strength
      and power to His people.
   Blessed be God!

PSALM 68:35

I sought the LORD, and He heard me,
   And delivered me from all my fears.

PSALM 34:4

"Fear not, for I am with you;
   Be not dismayed, for I am your God.
   I will strengthen you,
   Yes, I will help you,
   I will uphold you with My righteous
      right hand."

ISAIAH 41:10

Now, therefore, you are no longer strangers and foreigners, but fellow citizens with the saints and members of the household of God.

EPHESIANS 2:19

"Behold, I give you the authority to trample on serpents and scorpions, and over all the power of the enemy, and nothing shall by any means hurt you."

LUKE 10:19

My little children, let us not love in word or in tongue, but in deed and in truth. And by this we know that we are of the truth, and shall assure our hearts before Him. For if our heart condemns us, God is greater than our heart, and knows all things. Beloved, if our heart does not condemn us, we have confidence toward God. And whatever we ask we receive from Him, because we keep His commandments and do those things that are pleasing in His sight. And this is His commandment: that we should believe on the name of His Son Jesus Christ and love one another, as He gave us commandment.

1 JOHN 3:18–23

God's Answers *for* Me . . .

WHAT IS THE SECRET TO CHRIST-CENTERED RELATIONSHIPS?

❧─────────────────❧

I will sing of mercy and justice;
    To You, O LORD, I will sing praises.
I will behave wisely in a perfect way.
    Oh, when will You come to me?
    I will walk within my house with a
        perfect heart. . . .
My eyes shall be on the faithful of the land,
    That they may dwell with me;
    He who walks in a perfect way,
    He shall serve me.

PSALM 101:1–2, 6

"Take heed to yourselves. If your brother sins against you, rebuke him; and if he repents, forgive him. And if he sins against you seven times in a day, and seven times in a day returns to you, saying, 'I repent,' you shall forgive him."

LUKE 17:3–4

53

A soft answer turns away wrath,
But a harsh word stirs up anger.
The tongue of the wise uses knowledge rightly,
But the mouth of fools pours forth foolishness.
The eyes of the LORD are in every place,
Keeping watch on the evil and the good.
A wholesome tongue is a tree of life,
But perverseness in it breaks the spirit.
A fool despises his father's instruction,
But he who receives correction is prudent.

PROVERBS 15:1–5

And this is His commandment: that we should believe on the name of His Son Jesus Christ and love one another, as He gave us commandment.

1 JOHN 3:23

Let nothing be done through selfish ambition or conceit, but in lowliness of mind let each esteem others better than himself.

PHILIPPIANS 2:3

Be of the same mind toward one another. Do not set your mind on high things, but associate with the humble. Do not be wise in your own opinion.

ROMANS 12:16

Since you have purified your souls in obeying the truth through the Spirit in sincere love of the brethren, love one another fervently with a pure heart.

1 PETER 1:22

Beloved, let us love one another, for love is of God; and everyone who loves is born of God and knows God. He who does not love does not know God, for God is love. In this the love of God was manifested toward us, that God has sent His only begotten Son into the world, that we might live through Him. In this is love, not that we loved God, but that He loved us and sent His Son to be the propitiation for our sins. Beloved, if God so loved us, we also ought to love one another.

1 JOHN 4:7–11

God's Answers *for* Me . . .

HOW DO GODLY PRIORITIES LEAD TO WHAT IS IMPORTANT?

⊰────────────⊱

Commit your way to the LORD,
    Trust also in Him,
      And He shall bring it to pass.
He shall bring forth your righteousness as
        the light,
    And your justice as the noonday.

PSALM 37:5–6

When He had called the people to Himself, with His disciples also, He said to them, "Whoever desires to come after Me, let him deny himself, and take up his cross, and follow Me. For whoever desires to save his life will lose it, but whoever loses his life for My sake and the gospel's will save it. For what will it profit a man if he gains the whole world, and loses his own soul? Or what will a man give in exchange for his soul?"

MARK 8:34–37

You are witnesses, and God also, how devoutly and justly and blamelessly we behaved ourselves among you who believe; as you know how we exhorted, and comforted, and charged every one of you, as a father does his own children, that you would walk worthy of God who calls you into His own kingdom and glory.

1 THESSALONIANS 2:10–12

And I thank Christ Jesus our Lord who has enabled me, because He counted me faithful, putting me into the ministry, although I was formerly a blasphemer, a persecutor, and an insolent man; but I obtained mercy because I did it ignorantly in unbelief. And the grace of our Lord was exceedingly abundant, with faith and love which are in Christ Jesus. This is a faithful saying and worthy of all acceptance, that Christ Jesus came into the world to save sinners, of whom I am chief. However, for this reason I obtained mercy, that in me first Jesus Christ might show all long-suffering, as a pattern to those who are going to believe on Him for everlasting life.

1 TIMOTHY 1:12–16

And now, Israel, what does the LORD your God require of you, but to fear the LORD your God, to walk in all His ways and to love Him, to serve the LORD your God with all your heart and with all your soul, and to keep the commandments of the LORD and His statutes which I command you today for your good? Indeed heaven and the highest heavens belong to the LORD your God, also the earth with all that is in it. The LORD delighted only in your fathers, to love them; and He chose their descendants after them, you above all peoples, as it is this day.

DEUTERONOMY 10:12–15

God's Answers *for* Me . . .

How Do I Keep
from Worrying?

❧━━━━━━━━━━━━━━━━❧

Search me, O God, and know my heart;
    Try me, and know my anxieties;
And see if there is any wicked way in me,
    And lead me in the way everlasting.

Psalm 139:23–24

Be anxious for nothing, but in everything by
prayer and supplication, with thanksgiving, let
your requests be made known to God; and the
peace of God, which surpasses all understanding, will guard your hearts and minds through
Christ Jesus.

Philippians 4:6–7

Therefore humble yourselves under the mighty
hand of God, that He may exalt you in due time,
casting all your care upon Him, for He cares for
you.

1 Peter 5:6–7

"Look at the birds of the air, for they neither sow nor reap nor gather into barns; yet your heavenly Father feeds them. Are you not of more value than they? Which of you by worrying can add one cubit to his stature?

"So why do you worry about clothing? Consider the lilies of the field, how they grow: they neither toil nor spin; and yet I say to you that even Solomon in all his glory was not arrayed like one of these. Now if God so clothes the grass of the field, which today is, and tomorrow is thrown into the oven, will He not much more clothe you, O you of little faith?"

MATTHEW 6:26–30

Love has been perfected among us in this: that we may have boldness in the day of judgment; because as He is, so are we in this world. There is no fear in love; but perfect love casts out fear, because fear involves torment. But he who fears has not been made perfect in love. We love Him because He first loved us.

1 JOHN 4:17–19

"Therefore do not worry, saying, 'What shall we eat?' or 'What shall we drink?' or 'What shall we wear?' For after all these things the Gentiles seek. For your heavenly Father knows that you need all these things. But seek first the kingdom of God and His righteousness, and all these things shall be added to you."

MATTHEW 6:31–33

Anxiety in the heart of man causes depression,
But a good word makes it glad.

PROVERBS 12:25

God's Answers *for* Me . . .

HOW CAN I HAVE
A POWERFUL PRAYER LIFE?

"Call to Me, and I will answer you, and show you great and mighty things, which you do not know."

JEREMIAH 33:3

Hear me when I call, O God of my righteousness!
  You have relieved me in my distress;
  Have mercy on me, and hear my prayer.

PSALM 4:1

O LORD, God of my salvation,
  I have cried out day and night before You.
Let my prayer come before You;
  Incline Your ear to my cry.

PSALM 88:1–2

Rejoice always, pray without ceasing, in everything give thanks; for this is the will of God in Christ Jesus for you.

1 THESSALONIANS 5:16–18

Confess your trespasses to one another, and pray for one another, that you may be healed. The effective, fervent prayer of a righteous man avails much.

JAMES 5:16

Seek the LORD while He may be found,
 Call upon Him while He is near. . . .
Let him return to the LORD,
 And He will have mercy on him;
 And to our God,
 For He will abundantly pardon.

ISAIAH 55:6–7

I will love You, O LORD, my strength.
The LORD is my rock and my fortress and
  my deliverer;
 My God, my strength, in whom I will trust;
 My shield and the horn of my salvation,
  my stronghold.
I will call upon the LORD, who is worthy to
  be praised.

PSALM 18:1–3

God's Answers *for* Me . . .

HOW CAN I LIVE A LIFE OF EXCELLENCE?

I beseech you therefore, brethren, by the mercies of God, that you present your bodies a living sacrifice, holy, acceptable to God, which is your reasonable service. And do not be conformed to this world, but be transformed by the renewing of your mind, that you may prove what is that good and acceptable and perfect will of God.

ROMANS 12:1–2

Therefore, whether you eat or drink, or whatever you do, do all to the glory of God. Give no offense, either to the Jews or to the Greeks or to the church of God, just as I also please all men in all things, not seeking my own profit, but the profit of many, that they may be saved.

1 CORINTHIANS 10:31–33

Finally, brethren, whatever things are true, whatever things are noble, whatever things are just, whatever things are pure, whatever things are lovely, whatever things are of good report, if there is any virtue and if there is anything praiseworthy—meditate on these things. The things which you learned and received and heard and saw in me, these do, and the God of peace will be with you.

PHILIPPIANS 4:8–9

But what things were gain to me, these I have counted loss for Christ. Yet indeed I also count all things loss for the excellence of the knowledge of Christ Jesus my Lord, for whom I have suffered the loss of all things, and count them as rubbish, that I may gain Christ and be found in Him, not having my own righteousness, which is from the law, but that which is through faith in Christ, the righteousness which is from God by faith; that I may know Him and the power of His resurrection, and the fellowship of His sufferings, being conformed to His death, if, by any means, I may attain to the resurrection from the dead.

PHILIPPIANS 3:7–11

"Let your heart retain my words;
    Keep my commands, and live.
Get wisdom! Get understanding!
    Do not forget, nor turn away from the words
        of my mouth.
Do not forsake her, and she will preserve you;
    Love her, and she will keep you.
Wisdom is the principal thing;
    Therefore get wisdom.
    And in all your getting, get understanding.
Exalt her, and she will promote you;
    She will bring you honor, when you embrace
        her.
She will place on your head an ornament of grace;
    A crown of glory she will deliver to you."
Hear, my son, and receive my sayings,
    And the years of your life will be many.
I have taught you in the way of wisdom;
    I have led you in right paths.
When you walk, your steps will not be hindered,
    And when you run, you will not stumble.
Take firm hold of instruction, do not let go;
    Keep her, for she is your life.

PROVERBS 4:4–13

Listen, for I will speak of excellent things,
And from the opening of my lips will come
right things.

PROVERBS 8:6

And this I pray, that your love may abound still more and more in knowledge and all discernment, that you may approve the things that are excellent, that you may be sincere and without offense till the day of Christ, being filled with the fruits of righteousness which are by Jesus Christ, to the glory and praise of God.

PHILIPPIANS 1:9–11

God's Answers *for* Me . . .

How Do I Handle Disappointment?

※————————————❧

"Let not your heart be troubled; you believe in God, believe also in Me. In My Father's house are many mansions; if it were not so, I would have told you. I go to prepare a place for you. And if I go and prepare a place for you, I will come again and receive you to Myself; that where I am, there you may be also."

JOHN 14:1–3

Be anxious for nothing, but in everything by prayer and supplication, with thanksgiving, let your requests be made known to God; and the peace of God, which surpasses all understanding, will guard your hearts and minds through Christ Jesus.

PHILIPPIANS 4:6–7

For affliction does not come from the dust,
    Nor does trouble spring from the ground;
Yet man is born to trouble,
    As the sparks fly upward.
But as for me, I would seek God,
    And to God I would commit my cause—
Who does great things, and unsearchable,
    Marvelous things without number.
He gives rain on the earth,
    And sends waters on the fields.
He sets on high those who are lowly,
    And those who mourn are lifted to safety.

JOB 5:6–11

For I know that my Redeemer lives,
    And He shall stand at last on the earth;
And after my skin is destroyed, this I know,
    That in my flesh I shall see God,
Whom I shall see for myself,
    And my eyes shall behold, and not another.
    How my heart yearns within me!

JOB 19:25–27

The LORD is my light and my salvation;
  Whom shall I fear?
  The LORD is the strength of my life;
  Of whom shall I be afraid?
When the wicked came against me
  To eat up my flesh,
  My enemies and foes,
  They stumbled and fell.
Though an army may encamp against me,
  My heart shall not fear;
  Though war may rise against me,
  In this I will be confident.
One thing I have desired of the LORD,
  That will I seek:
  That I may dwell in the house of the LORD
  All the days of my life,
  To behold the beauty of the LORD,
  And to inquire in His temple.
For in the time of trouble
  He shall hide me in His pavilion;
  In the secret place of His tabernacle
  He shall hide me;
  He shall set me high upon a rock.

PSALM 27:1–5

God's Answers *for* Me . . .

HOW DOES GOD'S LOVE COVER MY SIN?

———————————————————

But God demonstrates His own love toward us, in that while we were still sinners, Christ died for us.

ROMANS 5:8

For all have sinned and fall short of the glory of God, being justified freely by His grace through the redemption that is in Christ Jesus, whom God set forth as a propitiation by His blood, through faith, to demonstrate His righteousness, because in His forbearance God had passed over the sins that were previously committed, to demonstrate at the present time His righteousness, that He might be just and the justifier of the one who has faith in Jesus.

ROMANS 3:23–26

In this is love, not that we loved God, but that He loved us and sent His Son to be the propitiation for our sins.

1 JOHN 4:10

"For this is My blood of the new covenant, which is shed for many for the remission of sins."

MATTHEW 26:28

My son, do not forget my law,
But let your heart keep my commands;
For length of days and long life
And peace they will add to you.
Let not mercy and truth forsake you;
Bind them around your neck,
Write them on the tablet of your heart,
And so find favor and high esteem
In the sight of God and man. . . .
My son, do not despise the chastening of
the LORD,
Nor detest His correction;
For whom the LORD loves He corrects,
Just as a father the son in whom he delights.

PROVERBS 3:1–4, 11–12

Hatred stirs up strife,
But love covers all sins.

PROVERBS 10:12

Grace to you and peace from Him who is and who was and who is to come, and from the seven Spirits who are before His throne, and from Jesus Christ, the faithful witness, the firstborn from the dead, and the ruler over the kings of the earth.

To Him who loved us and washed us from our sins in His own blood, and has made us kings and priests to His God and Father, to Him be glory and dominion forever and ever.

REVELATION 1:4–6

God's Answers *for* Me . . .

HOW DO I STAY CONNECTED TO GOD AFTER GRADUATION?

❦—————————————❧

Trust in the LORD with all your heart,
    And lean not on your own understanding;
In all your ways acknowledge Him,
    And He shall direct your paths.

PROVERBS 3:5–6

Trust in the LORD, and do good;
    Dwell in the land, and feed on His faithfulness.
Delight yourself also in the LORD,
    And He shall give you the desires of
        your heart.
Commit your way to the LORD,
    Trust also in Him,
    And He shall bring it to pass.
He shall bring forth your righteousness as
        the light,
    And your justice as the noonday.

PSALM 37:3–6

"I am the true vine, and My Father is the vine-dresser. Every branch in Me that does not bear fruit He takes away; and every branch that bears fruit He prunes, that it may bear more fruit. You are already clean because of the word which I have spoken to you. Abide in Me, and I in you. As the branch cannot bear fruit of itself, unless it abides in the vine, neither can you, unless you abide in Me.

"I am the vine, you are the branches. He who abides in Me, and I in him, bears much fruit; for without Me you can do nothing. If anyone does not abide in Me, he is cast out as a branch and is withered; and they gather them and throw them into the fire, and they are burned. If you abide in Me, and My words abide in you, you will ask what you desire, and it shall be done for you."

JOHN 15:1–7

Search me, O God, and know my heart;
    Try me, and know my anxieties;
And see if there is any wicked way in me,
    And lead me in the way everlasting.

PSALM 139:23–24

Be zealous for the fear of the LORD all the
    day;
For surely there is a hereafter,
    And your hope will not be cut off.

PROVERBS 23:17–18

The king shall have joy in Your strength, O LORD;
    And in Your salvation how greatly shall
        he rejoice!
You have given him his heart's desire,
    And have not withheld the request of his lips.
For You meet him with the blessings of goodness;
    You set a crown of pure gold upon his head.
He asked life from You, and You gave it to him—
    Length of days forever and ever.
His glory is great in Your salvation;
    Honor and majesty You have placed upon him.
For You have made him most blessed forever;
    You have made him exceedingly glad with
        Your presence.
For the king trusts in the LORD,
    And through the mercy of the Most High he
        shall not be moved.

PSALM 21:1–7

God's
Blessings
to Me . . .

God's Blessings *to* Me . . .

HIS LOVE IS CONSTANT

❧━━━━━━━━━━━━━━━━━━━━━━━❧

But the mercy of the LORD is from everlasting
       to everlasting
  On those who fear Him,
  And His righteousness to children's children.
PSALM 103:17

For I am persuaded that neither death nor life,
nor angels nor principalities nor powers, nor
things present nor things to come, nor height nor
depth, nor any other created thing, shall be able
to separate us from the love of God which is in
Christ Jesus our Lord.
ROMANS 8:38–39

Your kingdom is an everlasting kingdom,
  And Your dominion endures throughout
      all generations.
PSALM 145:13

Have you not known?
    Have you not heard?
    The everlasting God, the LORD,
    The Creator of the ends of the earth,
    Neither faints nor is weary.
    His understanding is unsearchable.

ISAIAH 40:28

For His merciful kindness is great toward us,
    And the truth of the LORD endures forever.
    Praise the LORD!

PSALM 117:2

God's Blessings *to* Me . . .

HE ENABLES ME TO LIVE VICTORIOUSLY

———————❧———————

"I have come that they may have life, and that they may have it more abundantly.

"I am the good shepherd. The good shepherd gives His life for the sheep."

JOHN 10:10–11

Who shall separate us from the love of Christ? Shall tribulation, or distress, or persecution, or famine, or nakedness, or peril, or sword? As it is written:

"For Your sake we are killed all day long;

We are accounted as sheep for the slaughter."

Yet in all these things we are more than conquerors through Him who loved us.

ROMANS 8:35–37

Now may the God of hope fill you with all joy and peace in believing, that you may abound in hope by the power of the Holy Spirit.

ROMANS 15:13

"Behold, I give you the authority to trample on serpents and scorpions, and over all the power of the enemy, and nothing shall by any means hurt you."

LUKE 10:19

Ascribe strength to God;
   His excellence is over Israel,
   And His strength is in the clouds.
O God, You are more awesome than Your
      holy places.
   The God of Israel is He who gives strength
      and power to His people.
   Blessed be God!

PSALM 68:34–35

Fight the good fight of faith, lay hold on eternal life, to which you were also called and have confessed the good confession in the presence of many witnesses.

1 TIMOTHY 6:12

"These things I have spoken to you, that in Me you may have peace. In the world you will have tribulation; but be of good cheer, I have overcome the world."

JOHN 16:33

For whatever is born of God overcomes the world. And this is the victory that has overcome the world—our faith. Who is he who overcomes the world, but he who believes that Jesus is the Son of God?

1 JOHN 5:4–5

The sting of death is sin, and the strength of sin is the law. But thanks be to God, who gives us the victory through our Lord Jesus Christ.

Therefore, my beloved brethren, be steadfast, immovable, always abounding in the work of the Lord, knowing that your labor is not in vain in the Lord.

1 CORINTHIANS 15:56–58

But I will sing of Your power;
　　Yes, I will sing aloud of Your mercy in
　　　　the morning;
　　For You have been my defense
　　And refuge in the day of my trouble.
To You, O my Strength, I will sing praises;
　　For God is my defense,
　　My God of mercy.

PSALM 59:16–17

And He said to me, "My grace is sufficient for you, for My strength is made perfect in weakness." Therefore most gladly I will rather boast in my infirmities, that the power of Christ may rest upon me.

2 CORINTHIANS 12:9

Now to Him who is able to do exceedingly abundantly above all that we ask or think, according to the power that works in us, to Him be glory in the church by Christ Jesus to all generations, forever and ever. Amen.

EPHESIANS 3:20–21

God's Blessings *to* Me . . .

HE WANTS ME TO
BELONG TO HIM

But now, thus says the LORD, who created you,
     O Jacob,
  And He who formed you, O Israel:
  "Fear not, for I have redeemed you;
  I have called you by your name;
  You are Mine.
When you pass through the waters, I will be
     with you;
  And through the rivers, they shall not
     overflow you.
  When you walk through the fire, you
     shall not be burned,
  Nor shall the flame scorch you.
For I am the LORD your God,
  The Holy One of Israel, your Savior."

ISAIAH 43:1–3

"To him the doorkeeper opens, and the sheep hear his voice; and he calls his own sheep by name and leads them out. And when he brings out his own sheep, he goes before them; and the sheep follow him, for they know his voice."

JOHN 10:3–4

Just as He chose us in Him before the foundation of the world, that we should be holy and without blame before Him in love, having predestined us to adoption as sons by Jesus Christ to Himself, according to the good pleasure of His will, to the praise of the glory of His grace, by which He made us accepted in the Beloved.

EPHESIANS 1:4–6

You were bought at a price; do not become slaves of men. Brethren, let each one remain with God in that state in which he was called.

1 CORINTHIANS 7:23–24

For this reason we also, since the day we heard it, do not cease to pray for you, and to ask that you may be filled with the knowledge of His will in all wisdom and spiritual understanding; that you may walk worthy of the Lord, fully pleasing Him, being fruitful in every good work and increasing in the knowledge of God; strengthened with all might, according to His glorious power, for all patience and longsuffering with joy; giving thanks to the Father who has qualified us to be partakers of the inheritance of the saints in the light.

COLOSSIANS 1:9–12

God's Blessings *to* Me . . .

HE WILL MEET MY NEEDS

───────────────────

I love the LORD, because He has heard
    My voice and my supplications.
Because He has inclined His ear to me,
    Therefore I will call upon Him as long as I live.
                                    PSALM 116:1–2

"Most assuredly, I say to you, whatever you ask
the Father in My name He will give you. Until
now you have asked nothing in My name. Ask,
and you will receive, that your joy may be full."
                                    JOHN 16:23–24

"For your Father knows the things you have need
of before you ask Him."

                                    MATTHEW 6:8

"For everyone who asks receives, and he who
seeks finds, and to him who knocks it will be
opened."

                                    LUKE 11:10

I will declare the decree:
   The LORD has said to Me,
   "You are My Son,
   Today I have begotten You.
Ask of Me, and I will give You
   The nations for Your inheritance,
   And the ends of the earth for Your
         possession."

PSALM 2:7–8

O LORD, You are my God.
   I will exalt You,
   I will praise Your name,
   For You have done wonderful things;
   Your counsels of old are faithfulness and truth. . . .
For You have been a strength to the poor,
   A strength to the needy in his distress,
   A refuge from the storm,
   A shade from the heat; . . .
And it will be said in that day:
   "Behold, this is our God;
   We have waited for Him, and He will save us.
   This is the LORD;
   We have waited for Him;
   We will be glad and rejoice in His salvation."

ISAIAH 25:1, 4, 9

So Jesus answered and said to them, "Have faith in God. For assuredly, I say to you, whoever says to this mountain, 'Be removed and be cast into the sea,' and does not doubt in his heart, but believes that those things he says will be done, he will have whatever he says. Therefore I say to you, whatever things you ask when you pray, believe that you receive them, and you will have them."

MARK 11:22–24

God is our refuge and strength,
    A very present help in trouble.
Therefore we will not fear,
    Even though the earth be removed,
    And though the mountains be carried into
        the midst of the sea;
Though its waters roar and be troubled,
    Though the mountains shake with its swelling.
There is a river whose streams shall make glad
        the city of God,
    The holy place of the tabernacle of the
        Most High.
God is in the midst of her, she shall not be moved;
    God shall help her, just at the break of dawn.

PSALM 46:1–5

God's Blessings *to* Me . . .

HE WILL GIVE ME GRACE

For the LORD God is a sun and shield;
   The LORD will give grace and glory;
   No good thing will He withhold
   From those who walk uprightly.
O LORD of hosts,
   Blessed is the man who trusts in You!

PSALM 84:11–12

Seeing then that we have a great High Priest who has passed through the heavens, Jesus the Son of God, let us hold fast our confession. For we do not have a High Priest who cannot sympathize with our weaknesses, but was in all points tempted as we are, yet without sin. Let us therefore come boldly to the throne of grace, that we may obtain mercy and find grace to help in time of need.

HEBREWS 4:14–16

In Him we have redemption through His blood, the forgiveness of sins, according to the riches of His grace which He made to abound toward us in all wisdom and prudence.

EPHESIANS 1:7–8

For the grace of God that brings salvation has appeared to all men, teaching us that, denying ungodliness and worldly lusts, we should live soberly, righteously, and godly in the present age, looking for the blessed hope and glorious appearing of our great God and Savior Jesus Christ, who gave Himself for us, that He might redeem us from every lawless deed and purify for Himself His own special people, zealous for good works.

TITUS 2:11–14

For all things are for your sakes, that grace, having spread through the many, may cause thanksgiving to abound to the glory of God.

2 CORINTHIANS 4:15

For the law was given through Moses, but grace and truth came through Jesus Christ.

JOHN 1:17

But when the kindness and the love of God our Savior toward man appeared, not by works of righteousness which we have done, but according to His mercy He saved us, through the washing of regeneration and renewing of the Holy Spirit, whom He poured out on us abundantly through Jesus Christ our Savior, that having been justified by His grace we should become heirs according to the hope of eternal life.

TITUS 3:4–7

God's Blessings *to* Me . . .

HE HAS GIVEN ME HIS HOLY SPIRIT

"These things I have spoken to you while being present with you. But the Helper, the Holy Spirit, whom the Father will send in My name, He will teach you all things, and bring to your remembrance all things that I said to you."

JOHN 14:25–26

Now hope does not disappoint, because the love of God has been poured out in our hearts by the Holy Spirit who was given to us.

ROMANS 5:5

I say then: Walk in the Spirit, and you shall not fulfill the lust of the flesh. For the flesh lusts against the Spirit, and the Spirit against the flesh; and these are contrary to one another, so that you do not do the things that you wish. But if you are led by the Spirit, you are not under the law.

GALATIANS 5:16–18

"But you shall receive power when the Holy Spirit has come upon you; and you shall be witnesses to Me in Jerusalem, and in all Judea and Samaria, and to the end of the earth."

ACTS 1:8

This Jesus God has raised up, of which we are all witnesses. Therefore being exalted to the right hand of God, and having received from the Father the promise of the Holy Spirit, He poured out this which you now see and hear.

ACTS 2:32–33

Now He who establishes us with you in Christ and has anointed us is God, who also has sealed us and given us the Spirit in our hearts as a guarantee.

2 CORINTHIANS 1:21–22

I indeed baptize you with water unto repentance, but He who is coming after me is mightier than I, whose sandals I am not worthy to carry. He will baptize you with the Holy Spirit and fire.

MATTHEW 3:11

God
Will Give
Hope . . .

God *Will* Give Hope . . .

WHEN I AM LONELY

❧━━━━━━━━━━━━━━━━━━━━❧

Be strong and of good courage, do not fear nor be afraid of them; for the LORD your God, He is the One who goes with you. He will not leave you nor forsake you.

DEUTERONOMY 31:6

"Fear not, for I am with you;
    Be not dismayed, for I am your God.
    I will strengthen you,
    Yes, I will help you,
    I will uphold you with My righteous
        right hand."

ISAIAH 41:10

And my God shall supply all your need according to His riches in glory by Christ Jesus.

PHILIPPIANS 4:19

The LORD will give strength to His people;
    The LORD will bless His people with peace.

PSALM 29:11

Yea, though I walk through the valley of the
      shadow of death,
   I will fear no evil;
   For You are with me;
   Your rod and Your staff, they comfort me.

PSALM 23:4

Now she who is really a widow, and left alone,
trusts in God and continues in supplications and
prayers night and day.

1 TIMOTHY 5:5

God *Will* Give Hope . . .

WHEN I AM WORRIED

※————————————————※

You will keep him in perfect peace,
    Whose mind is stayed on You,
    Because he trusts in You.
Trust in the LORD forever,
    For in YAH, the LORD, is everlasting strength.

ISAIAH 26:3–4

"Therefore do not worry, saying, 'What shall we eat?' or 'What shall we drink?' or 'What shall we wear?' For after all these things the Gentiles seek. For your heavenly Father knows that you need all these things. But seek first the kingdom of God and His righteousness, and all these things shall be added to you. Therefore do not worry about tomorrow, for tomorrow will worry about its own things. Sufficient for the day is its own trouble."

MATTHEW 6:31–34

"Peace I leave with you, My peace I give to you; not as the world gives do I give to you. Let not your heart be troubled, neither let it be afraid."

JOHN 14:27

Be anxious for nothing, but in everything by prayer and supplication, with thanksgiving, let your requests be made known to God; and the peace of God, which surpasses all understanding, will guard your hearts and minds through Christ Jesus.

PHILIPPIANS 4:6–7

"Therefore I say to you, do not worry about your life, what you will eat or what you will drink; nor about your body, what you will put on. Is not life more than food and the body more than clothing? Look at the birds of the air, for they neither sow nor reap nor gather into barns; yet your heavenly Father feeds them. Are you not of more value than they? Which of you by worrying can add one cubit to his stature?"

MATTHEW 6:25–27

"Consider the lilies, how they grow: they neither toil nor spin; and yet I say to you, even Solomon in all his glory was not arrayed like one of these. If then God so clothes the grass, which today is in the field and tomorrow is thrown into the oven, how much more will He clothe you, O you of little faith?"

LUKE 12:27–28

God *Will* Give Hope . . .

WHEN I AM DEPRESSED

He heals the brokenhearted
   And binds up their wounds.
He counts the number of the stars;
   He calls them all by name.
Great is our Lord, and mighty in power;
   His understanding is infinite.
The LORD lifts up the humble.

PSALM 147:3–6

He gives power to the weak,
   And to those who have no might He
      increases strength.
Even the youths shall faint and be weary,
   And the young men shall utterly fall,
But those who wait on the LORD
   Shall renew their strength;
   They shall mount up with wings like eagles,
   They shall run and not be weary,
   They shall walk and not faint.

ISAIAH 40:29–31

Blessed be the God and Father of our Lord Jesus Christ, the Father of mercies and God of all comfort, who comforts us in all our tribulation, that we may be able to comfort those who are in any trouble, with the comfort with which we ourselves are comforted by God.

2 Corinthians 1:3–4

Beloved, do not think it strange concerning the fiery trial which is to try you, as though some strange thing happened to you; but rejoice to the extent that you partake of Christ's sufferings, that when His glory is revealed, you may also be glad with exceeding joy. If you are reproached for the name of Christ, blessed are you, for the Spirit of glory and of God rests upon you. On their part He is blasphemed, but on your part He is glorified.

1 Peter 4:12–14

Why are you cast down, O my soul?
　　And why are you disquieted within me?
　　Hope in God, for I shall yet praise Him
　　For the help of His countenance.

Psalm 42:5

But we have this treasure in earthen vessels, that the excellence of the power may be of God and not of us. We are hard-pressed on every side, yet not crushed; we are perplexed, but not in despair . . . struck down, but not destroyed—always carrying about in the body the dying of the Lord Jesus, that the life of Jesus also may be manifested in our body.

2 Corinthians 4:7–10

Enter into His gates with thanksgiving,
    And into His courts with praise.
    Be thankful to Him, and bless His name.
For the Lord is good;
    His mercy is everlasting,
    And His truth endures to all generations.

Psalm 100:4–5

God *Will* Give Hope . . .

WHEN I AM GUILTY

I acknowledged my sin to You,
 And my iniquity I have not hidden.
 I said, "I will confess my transgressions to
   the LORD,"
 And You forgave the iniquity of my sin. . . .
You are my hiding place;
 You shall preserve me from trouble;
 You shall surround me with songs
   of deliverance.

PSALM 32:5, 7

"For God did not send His Son into the world to condemn the world, but that the world through Him might be saved.

"He who believes in Him is not condemned; but he who does not believe is condemned already, because he has not believed in the name of the only begotten Son of God."

JOHN 3:17–18

If we say that we have no sin, we deceive ourselves, and the truth is not in us. If we confess our sins, He is faithful and just to forgive us our sins and to cleanse us from all unrighteousness.

1 JOHN 1:8–9

Then I heard a loud voice saying in heaven, "Now salvation, and strength, and the kingdom of our God, and the power of His Christ have come, for the accuser of our brethren, who accused them before our God day and night, has been cast down."

REVELATION 12:10

For all have sinned and fall short of the glory of God, being justified freely by His grace through the redemption that is in Christ Jesus, whom God set forth as a propitiation by His blood, through faith, to demonstrate His righteousness, because in His forbearance God had passed over the sins that were previously committed, to demonstrate at the present time His righteousness, that He might be just and the justifier of the one who has faith in Jesus.

ROMANS 3:23–26

God *Will* Give Hope . . .

WHEN I AM CONFUSED

———————❧———————

I will instruct you and teach you in the way
      you should go;
   I will guide you with My eye.

PSALM 32:8

Trust in the LORD with all your heart,
   And lean not on your own understanding;
In all your ways acknowledge Him,
   And He shall direct your paths.

PROVERBS 3:5–6

For where envy and self-seeking exist, confusion
and every evil thing are there. But the wisdom
that is from above is first pure, then peaceable,
gentle, willing to yield, full of mercy and good
fruits, without partiality and without hypocrisy.
Now the fruit of righteousness is sown in peace
by those who make peace.

JAMES 3:16–18

For God is not the author of confusion but of peace, as in all the churches of the saints.

1 CORINTHIANS 14:33

Trust in the LORD, and do good;
    Dwell in the land, and feed on His faithfulness.
Delight yourself also in the LORD,
    And He shall give you the desires of your heart.
Commit your way to the LORD,
    Trust also in Him,
    And He shall bring it to pass.
He shall bring forth your righteousness as
        the light,
    And your justice as the noonday.

PSALM 37:3–6

"For I know the thoughts that I think toward you, says the LORD, thoughts of peace and not of evil, to give you a future and a hope. Then you will call upon Me and go and pray to Me, and I will listen to you. And you will seek Me and find Me, when you search for Me with all your heart."

JEREMIAH 29:11–13

God *Will* Give Hope . . .

WHEN I AM TEMPTED

❧────────────────────❧

No temptation has overtaken you except such as is common to man; but God is faithful, who will not allow you to be tempted beyond what you are able, but with the temptation will also make the way of escape, that you may be able to bear it.

1 CORINTHIANS 10:13

How can a young man cleanse his way?
  By taking heed according to Your word.
With my whole heart I have sought You;
    Oh, let me not wander from Your
        commandments!
Your word I have hidden in my heart,
    That I might not sin against You.
Blessed are You, O LORD!
    Teach me Your statutes.

PSALM 119:9–12

For we do not have a High Priest who cannot sympathize with our weaknesses, but was in all points tempted as we are, yet without sin. Let us therefore come boldly to the throne of grace, that we may obtain mercy and find grace to help in time of need.

HEBREWS 4:15–16

Put on the whole armor of God, that you may be able to stand against the wiles of the devil. For we do not wrestle against flesh and blood, but against principalities, against powers, against the rulers of the darkness of this age, against spiritual hosts of wickedness in the heavenly places. Therefore take up the whole armor of God, that you may be able to withstand in the evil day, and having done all, to stand.

Stand therefore, having girded your waist with truth, having put on the breastplate of righteousness, and having shod your feet with the preparation of the gospel of peace; above all, taking the shield of faith with which you will be able to quench all the fiery darts of the wicked one. And take the helmet of salvation, and the sword of the Spirit, which is the word of God.

EPHESIANS 6:11–17

Then Jesus was led up by the Spirit into the wilderness to be tempted by the devil. And when He had fasted forty days and forty nights, afterward He was hungry. Now when the tempter came to Him, he said, "If You are the Son of God, command that these stones become bread."

But He answered and said, "It is written, 'Man shall not live by bread alone, but by every word that proceeds from the mouth of God.'"

Then the devil took Him up into the holy city, set Him on the pinnacle of the temple, and said to Him, "If You are the Son of God, throw Yourself down. For it is written:

'He shall give His angels charge over you,'
    and,
'In their hands they shall bear you up,
Lest you dash your foot against a stone.'"

Jesus said to him, "It is written again, 'You shall not tempt the LORD your God.'"

Again, the devil took Him up on an exceedingly high mountain, and showed Him all the kingdoms of the world and their glory. And he said to Him, "All these things I will give You if You will fall down and worship me."

Then Jesus said to him, "Away with you, Satan! For it is written, 'You shall worship the LORD your God, and Him only you shall serve.'"

MATTHEW 4:1–10

Let no one say when he is tempted, "I am tempted by God"; for God cannot be tempted by evil, nor does He Himself tempt anyone. But each one is tempted when he is drawn away by his own desires and enticed.

JAMES 1:13–14

God *Will* Give Hope . . .

WHEN I AM ANGRY

Rest in the LORD, and wait patiently for Him;
    Do not fret because of him who prospers in
        his way,
    Because of the man who brings wicked
        schemes to pass.
Cease from anger, and forsake wrath;
    Do not fret—it only causes harm.

PSALM 37:7–8

A soft answer turns away wrath,
    But a harsh word stirs up anger.
The tongue of the wise uses knowledge rightly,
    But the mouth of fools pours forth foolishness.

PROVERBS 15:1–2

"Be angry, and do not sin": do not let the sun go
down on your wrath, nor give place to the devil.

EPHESIANS 4:26–27

Let no corrupt word proceed out of your mouth, but what is good for necessary edification, that it may impart grace to the hearers. And do not grieve the Holy Spirit of God, by whom you were sealed for the day of redemption. Let all bitterness, wrath, anger, clamor, and evil speaking be put away from you, with all malice.

EPHESIANS 4:29–31

An angry man stirs up strife,
And a furious man abounds in transgression.

PROVERBS 29:22

So then, my beloved brethren, let every man be swift to hear, slow to speak, slow to wrath; for the wrath of man does not produce the righteousness of God.

Therefore lay aside all filthiness and overflow of wickedness, and receive with meekness the implanted word, which is able to save your souls.

JAMES 1:19–21

God *Will* Give Hope . . .

WHEN I FEEL REJECTED

But the LORD said to Samuel, "Do not look at his appearance or at his physical stature, because I have refused him. For the LORD does not see as man sees; for man looks at the outward appearance, but the LORD looks at the heart."

1 SAMUEL 16:7

The righteous cry out, and the LORD hears,
    And delivers them out of all their troubles.
The LORD is near to those who have a
        broken heart,
    And saves such as have a contrite spirit.
Many are the afflictions of the righteous,
    But the LORD delivers him out of them all.

PSALM 34:17–19

Blessed be God,
    Who has not turned away my prayer,
    Nor His mercy from me!

PSALM 66:20

He is despised and rejected by men,
    A Man of sorrows and acquainted with grief.
    And we hid, as it were, our faces from Him;
    He was despised, and we did not esteem Him.
Surely He has borne our griefs
    And carried our sorrows;
    Yet we esteemed Him stricken,
    Smitten by God, and afflicted.
But He was wounded for our transgressions,
    He was bruised for our iniquities;
    The chastisement for our peace was upon Him,
    And by His stripes we are healed.

ISAIAH 53:3–5

Coming to Him as to a living stone, rejected indeed by men, but chosen by God and precious, you also, as living stones, are being built up a spiritual house, a holy priesthood, to offer up spiritual sacrifices acceptable to God through Jesus Christ.

1 PETER 2:4–5

God *Will* Give Hope . . .

When I Am Rebellious

───────────────────

There is a way that seems right to a man,
　　But its end is the way of death.
Even in laughter the heart may sorrow,
　　And the end of mirth may be grief.
The backslider in heart will be filled with his
　　　　own ways,
　　But a good man will be satisfied from above.

PROVERBS 14:12–14

"What man of you, having a hundred sheep, if he loses one of them, does not leave the ninety-nine in the wilderness, and go after the one which is lost until he finds it? And when he has found it, he lays it on his shoulders, rejoicing. And when he comes home, he calls together his friends and neighbors, saying to them, 'Rejoice with me, for I have found my sheep which was lost!' I say to you that likewise there will be more joy in heaven over one sinner who repents than over ninety-nine just persons who need no repentance."

LUKE 15:4–7

Finally, all of you be of one mind, having compassion for one another; love as brothers, be tenderhearted, be courteous; not returning evil for evil or reviling for reviling, but on the contrary blessing, knowing that you were called to this, that you may inherit a blessing. For

"He who would love life
And see good days,
Let him refrain his tongue from evil,
And his lips from speaking deceit.
Let him turn away from evil and do good;
Let him seek peace and pursue it."

1 PETER 3:8–11

Remember those who rule over you, who have spoken the word of God to you, whose faith follow, considering the outcome of their conduct. . . . Obey those who rule over you, and be submissive, for they watch out for your souls, as those who must give account. Let them do so with joy and not with grief, for that would be unprofitable for you.

HEBREWS 13:7, 17

These things indeed have an appearance of wisdom in self-imposed religion, false humility, and neglect of the body, but are of no value against the indulgence of the flesh.

COLOSSIANS 2:23

For He is our God,
And we are the people of His pasture,
And the sheep of His hand.
Today, if you will hear His voice:
"Do not harden your hearts, as in the
rebellion,
As in the day of trial in the wilderness."

PSALM 95:7–8

Likewise you younger people, submit yourselves to your elders. Yes, all of you be submissive to one another, and be clothed with humility, for
"God resists the proud,
But gives grace to the humble."
Therefore humble yourselves under the mighty hand of God, that He may exalt you in due time.

1 PETER 5:5–6

God *Will* Give Hope . . .

WHEN I DON'T FEEL IMPORTANT

For as the body is one and has many members, but all the members of that one body, being many, are one body, so also is Christ. . . .

If the foot should say, "Because I am not a hand, I am not of the body," is it therefore not of the body? And if the ear should say, "Because I am not an eye, I am not of the body," is it therefore not of the body? If the whole body were an eye, where would be the hearing? If the whole were hearing, where would be the smelling? But now God has set the members, each one of them, in the body just as He pleased. And if they were all one member, where would the body be?

But now indeed there are many members, yet one body. And the eye cannot say to the hand, "I have no need of you"; nor again the head to the feet, "I have no need of you." No, much rather, those members of the body which seem to be weaker are necessary. And those members of the body which we think to be less honorable, on these we bestow greater honor; and our unpresentable parts have greater modesty, but our presentable parts have no need. But God composed the body, having given greater honor to that part which lacks it, that there should be no schism in the body, but that the members should have the same care for one another. And if one member suffers, all the members suffer with it; or if one member is honored, all the members rejoice with it.

1 CORINTHIANS 12:12, 15–26

For thus says the LORD of hosts: "He sent Me after glory, to the nations which plunder you; for he who touches you touches the apple of His eye. For surely I will shake My hand against them, and they shall become spoil for their servants. Then you will know that the LORD of hosts has sent Me."

ZECHARIAH 2:8–9

I will praise You, for I am fearfully and
      wonderfully made;
  Marvelous are Your works,
  And that my soul knows very well.

PSALM 139:14

God
will Help
Me . . .

God *Will* Help Me . . .

PRAY EFFECTIVELY

⚜━━━━━━━━━━━⚜

Be anxious for nothing, but in everything by prayer and supplication, with thanksgiving, let your requests be made known to God; and the peace of God, which surpasses all understanding, will guard your hearts and minds through Christ Jesus.

PHILIPPIANS 4:6–7

"Call to Me, and I will answer you, and show you great and mighty things, which you do not know."

JEREMIAH 33:3

Confess your trespasses to one another, and pray for one another, that you may be healed. The effective, fervent prayer of a righteous man avails much.

JAMES 5:16

Evening and morning and at noon
   I will pray, and cry aloud,
   And He shall hear my voice.

PSALM 55:17

"So I say to you, ask, and it will be given to you; seek, and you will find; knock, and it will be opened to you. For everyone who asks receives, and he who seeks finds, and to him who knocks it will be opened."

LUKE 11:9–10

"Assuredly, I say to you, whatever you bind on earth will be bound in heaven, and whatever you loose on earth will be loosed in heaven.

"Again I say to you that if two of you agree on earth concerning anything that they ask, it will be done for them by My Father in heaven."

MATTHEW 18:18–19

"And when you pray, you shall not be like the hypocrites. For they love to pray standing in the synagogues and on the corners of the streets, that they may be seen by men. Assuredly, I say to you, they have their reward. But you, when you pray, go into your room, and when you have shut your door, pray to your Father who is in the secret place; and your Father who sees in secret will reward you openly."

MATTHEW 6:5–6

"In this manner, therefore, pray:
    Our Father in heaven,
    Hallowed be Your name.
    Your kingdom come.
    Your will be done
    On earth as it is in heaven.
    Give us this day our daily bread.
    And forgive us our debts,
    As we forgive our debtors.
    And do not lead us into temptation,
    But deliver us from the evil one.
    For Yours is the kingdom and the power and
        the glory forever. Amen."

MATTHEW 6:9–13

God *Will* Help Me . . .

SHARE MY TESTIMONY

❧━━━━━━━━━━━━━━━━━❧

"You are the light of the world. A city that is set on a hill cannot be hidden. Nor do they light a lamp and put it under a basket, but on a lampstand, and it gives light to all who are in the house. Let your light so shine before men, that they may see your good works and glorify your Father in heaven."

MATTHEW 5:14–16

"No one, when he has lit a lamp, puts it in a secret place or under a basket, but on a lampstand, that those who come in may see the light. The lamp of the body is the eye. Therefore, when your eye is good, your whole body also is full of light. But when your eye is bad, your body also is full of darkness. Therefore take heed that the light which is in you is not darkness. If then your whole body is full of light, having no part dark, the whole body will be full of light, as when the bright shining of a lamp gives you light."

LUKE 11:33–36

And take the helmet of salvation, and the sword of the Spirit, which is the word of God; praying always with all prayer and supplication in the Spirit, being watchful to this end with all perseverance and supplication for all the saints—and for me, that utterance may be given to me, that I may open my mouth boldly to make known the mystery of the gospel, for which I am an ambassador in chains; that in it I may speak boldly, as I ought to speak.

EPHESIANS 6:17–20

Then Moses said to the LORD, "O my Lord, I am not eloquent, neither before nor since You have spoken to Your servant; but I am slow of speech and slow of tongue."

So the LORD said to him, "Who has made man's mouth? Or who makes the mute, the deaf, the seeing, or the blind? Have not I, the LORD? Now therefore, go, and I will be with your mouth and teach you what you shall say."

EXODUS 4:10–12

"Also I say to you, whoever confesses Me before men, him the Son of Man also will confess before the angels of God."

LUKE 12:8

But sanctify the Lord God in your hearts, and always be ready to give a defense to everyone who asks you a reason for the hope that is in you, with meekness and fear; having a good conscience, that when they defame you as evildoers, those who revile your good conduct in Christ may be ashamed. For it is better, if it is the will of God, to suffer for doing good than for doing evil.

1 PETER 3:15–17

Then he said, "The God of our fathers has chosen you that you should know His will, and see the Just One, and hear the voice of His mouth. For you will be His witness to all men of what you have seen and heard."

ACTS 22:14–15

And this I pray, that your love may abound still more and more in knowledge and all discernment, that you may approve the things that are excellent, that you may be sincere and without offense till the day of Christ, being filled with the fruits of righteousness which are by Jesus Christ, to the glory and praise of God.

PHILIPPIANS 1:9–11

God *Will* Help Me . . .

UNDERSTAND HIS WILL

"The LORD will guide you continually,
   And satisfy your soul in drought,
   And strengthen your bones;
   You shall be like a watered garden,
   And like a spring of water, whose waters
      do not fail.
Those from among you
   Shall build the old waste places;
   You shall raise up the foundations of
      many generations;
   And you shall be called the Repairer of
      the Breach,
   The Restorer of Streets to Dwell In."

ISAIAH 58:11–12

Your testimonies are wonderful;
   Therefore my soul keeps them.
The entrance of Your words gives light;
   It gives understanding to the simple.

PSALM 119:129–130

When a man's ways please the LORD,
   He makes even his enemies to be at peace
      with him.
Better is a little with righteousness,
   Than vast revenues without justice.
A man's heart plans his way,
   But the LORD directs his steps.

PROVERBS 16:7–9

Then He said to them, "These are the words which I spoke to you while I was still with you, that all things must be fulfilled which were written in the Law of Moses and the Prophets and the Psalms concerning Me." And He opened their understanding, that they might comprehend the Scriptures.

LUKE 24:44–45

The fear of the LORD is the beginning of wisdom;
   A good understanding have all those who do
      His commandments.
   His praise endures forever.

PSALM 111:10

Who is wise and understanding among you? Let him show by good conduct that his works are done in the meekness of wisdom.

JAMES 3:13

And we know that the Son of God has come and has given us an understanding, that we may know Him who is true; and we are in Him who is true, in His Son Jesus Christ. This is the true God and eternal life.

1 JOHN 5:20

God *Will* Help Me . . .

PRIORITIZE MY FINANCES

But this I say: He who sows sparingly will also reap sparingly, and he who sows bountifully will also reap bountifully. So let each one give as he purposes in his heart, not grudgingly or of necessity; for God loves a cheerful giver.

2 CORINTHIANS 9:6–7

"Bring all the tithes into the storehouse,
   That there may be food in My house,
   And try Me now in this,"
   Says the LORD of hosts,
   "If I will not open for you the windows
         of heaven
   And pour out for you such blessing
   That there will not be room enough to
         receive it."

MALACHI 3:10

He who has a generous eye will be blessed,
   For he gives of his bread to the poor.

PROVERBS 22:9

"Give, and it will be given to you: good measure, pressed down, shaken together, and running over will be put into your bosom. For with the same measure that you use, it will be measured back to you."

LUKE 6:38

Lest you learn his ways
   And set a snare for your soul.
Do not be one of those who shakes hands in a
      pledge,
   One of those who is surety for debts;
If you have nothing with which to pay,
   Why should he take away your bed from
      under you?
Do not remove the ancient landmark
   Which your fathers have set.

PROVERBS 22:25–28

"Do not lay up for yourselves treasures on earth, where moth and rust destroy and where thieves break in and steal; but lay up for yourselves treasures in heaven, where neither moth nor rust destroys and where thieves do not break in and steal. For where your treasure is, there your heart will be also."

MATTHEW 6:19–21

"If he has not oppressed anyone,
    But has restored to the debtor his pledge;
    Has robbed no one by violence,
    But has given his bread to the hungry
    And covered the naked with clothing;
If he has not exacted usury
    Nor taken any increase,
    But has withdrawn his hand from iniquity
    And executed true judgment between man
            and man;
If he has walked in My statutes
    And kept My judgments faithfully—
    He is just;
    He shall surely live!"
    Says the Lord GOD.

Ezekiel 18:7–9

"He who is faithful in what is least is faithful also in much; and he who is unjust in what is least is unjust also in much. Therefore if you have not been faithful in the unrighteous mammon, who will commit to your trust the true riches?"

Luke 16:10–11

Owe no one anything except to love one another, for he who loves another has fulfilled the law.

ROMANS 13:8

Now may He who supplies seed to the sower, and bread for food, supply and multiply the seed you have sown and increase the fruits of your righteousness, while you are enriched in everything for all liberality, which causes thanksgiving through us to God. For the administration of this service not only supplies the needs of the saints, but also is abounding through many thanksgivings to God, while, through the proof of this ministry, they glorify God for the obedience of your confession to the gospel of Christ, and for your liberal sharing with them and all men.

2 CORINTHIANS 9:10–13

God *Will* Help Me . . .

UNDERSTAND HIS WORD

For the word of God is living and powerful, and sharper than any two-edged sword, piercing even to the division of soul and spirit, and of joints and marrow, and is a discerner of the thoughts and intents of the heart.

HEBREWS 4:12

"This Book of the Law shall not depart from your mouth, but you shall meditate in it day and night, that you may observe to do according to all that is written in it. For then you will make your way prosperous, and then you will have good success. Have I not commanded you? Be strong and of good courage; do not be afraid, nor be dismayed, for the LORD your God is with you wherever you go."

JOSHUA 1:8–9

But He answered and said, "It is written, 'Man shall not live by bread alone, but by every word that proceeds from the mouth of God.'"

MATTHEW 4:4

How sweet are Your words to my taste,
  Sweeter than honey to my mouth!
Through Your precepts I get understanding;
  Therefore I hate every false way.
Your word is a lamp to my feet
  And a light to my path.

PSALM 119:103–105

Since you have purified your souls in obeying the truth through the Spirit in sincere love of the brethren, love one another fervently with a pure heart, having been born again, not of corruptible seed but incorruptible, through the word of God which lives and abides forever, because

  "All flesh is as grass,
  And all the glory of man as the flower of
      the grass.
  The grass withers,
  And its flower falls away,
  But the word of the LORD endures forever."
  Now this is the word which by the gospel was preached to you.

1 PETER 1:22–25

God *Will* Help Me . . .

HAVE A CLOSER WALK
WITH CHRIST

———————⚜———————

"Abide in Me, and I in you. As the branch cannot bear fruit of itself, unless it abides in the vine, neither can you, unless you abide in Me.

"I am the vine, you are the branches. He who abides in Me, and I in him, bears much fruit; for without Me you can do nothing. If anyone does not abide in Me, he is cast out as a branch and is withered; and they gather them and throw them into the fire, and they are burned. If you abide in Me, and My words abide in you, you will ask what you desire, and it shall be done for you."

JOHN 15:4–7

Let the word of Christ dwell in you richly in all wisdom, teaching and admonishing one another in psalms and hymns and spiritual songs, singing with grace in your hearts to the Lord.

COLOSSIANS 3:16

"My sheep hear My voice, and I know them, and they follow Me."

JOHN 10:27

"I am the light of the world. He who follows Me shall not walk in darkness, but have the light of life."

JOHN 8:12

And now, little children, abide in Him, that when He appears, we may have confidence and not be ashamed before Him at His coming.

1 JOHN 2:28

Blessed is the man who listens to me,
    Watching daily at my gates,
    Waiting at the posts of my doors.

PROVERBS 8:34

Now by this we know that we know Him, if we keep His commandments. He who says, "I know Him," and does not keep His commandments, is a liar, and the truth is not in him. But whoever keeps His word, truly the love of God is perfected in him. By this we know that we are in Him. He who says he abides in Him ought himself also to walk just as He walked.

1 JOHN 2:3–6

Blessed is the man
Who walks not in the counsel of the ungodly,
    Nor stands in the path of sinners,
    Nor sits in the seat of the scornful;
But his delight is in the law of the LORD,
    And in His law he meditates day and night.
He shall be like a tree
    Planted by the rivers of water,
    That brings forth its fruit in its season,
    Whose leaf also shall not wither;
And whatever he does shall prosper.

PSALM 1:1–3

So Jesus said to them, "Assuredly I say to you, that in the regeneration, when the Son of Man sits on the throne of His glory, you who have followed Me will also sit on twelve thrones, judging the twelve tribes of Israel. And everyone who has left houses or brothers or sisters or father or mother or wife or children or lands, for My name's sake, shall receive a hundredfold, and inherit eternal life."

MATTHEW 19:28–29

God *Will* Help Me . . .

BUILD MY FAITH

Now faith is the substance of things hoped for, the evidence of things not seen. . . .

By faith we understand that the worlds were framed by the word of God, so that the things which are seen were not made of things which are visible. . . .

But without faith it is impossible to please Him, for he who comes to God must believe that He is, and that He is a rewarder of those who diligently seek Him.

HEBREWS 11:1, 3, 6

If any of you lacks wisdom, let him ask of God, who gives to all liberally and without reproach, and it will be given to him. But let him ask in faith, with no doubting, for he who doubts is like a wave of the sea driven and tossed by the wind. For let not that man suppose that he will receive anything from the Lord; he is a double-minded man, unstable in all his ways.

JAMES 1:5–8

Blessed be the God and Father of our Lord Jesus Christ, who according to His abundant mercy has begotten us again to a living hope through the resurrection of Jesus Christ from the dead, to an inheritance incorruptible and undefiled and that does not fade away, reserved in heaven for you, who are kept by the power of God through faith for salvation ready to be revealed in the last time.

In this you greatly rejoice, though now for a little while, if need be, you have been grieved by various trials, that the genuineness of your faith, being much more precious than gold that perishes, though it is tested by fire, may be found to praise, honor, and glory at the revelation of Jesus Christ, whom having not seen you love. Though now you do not see Him, yet believing, you rejoice with joy inexpressible and full of glory, receiving the end of your faith—the salvation of your souls.

1 PETER 1:3–9

So then faith comes by hearing, and hearing by the word of God.

ROMANS 10:17

141

He did not waver at the promise of God through unbelief, but was strengthened in faith, giving glory to God, and being fully convinced that what He had promised He was also able to perform. And therefore "it was accounted to him for righteousness."

Romans 4:20–22

What does it profit, my brethren, if someone says he has faith but does not have works? Can faith save him? If a brother or sister is naked and destitute of daily food, and one of you says to them, "Depart in peace, be warmed and filled," but you do not give them the things which are needed for the body, what does it profit? Thus also faith by itself, if it does not have works, is dead.

But someone will say, "You have faith, and I have works." Show me your faith without your works, and I will show you my faith by my works.

James 2:14–18

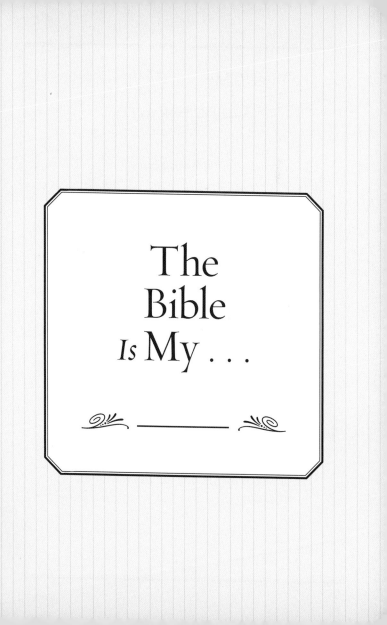

The
Bible
Is My . . .

The Bible *Is* My . . .

GUIDE FOR LIFE

❧———————————————————☙

All Scripture is given by inspiration of God, and is profitable for doctrine, for reproof, for correction, for instruction in righteousness, that the man of God may be complete, thoroughly equipped for every good work.

2 TIMOTHY 3:16–17

My son, keep your father's command,
    And do not forsake the law of your mother.
Bind them continually upon your heart;
    Tie them around your neck.
When you roam, they will lead you;
    When you sleep, they will keep you;
    And when you awake, they will speak
        with you.
For the commandment is a lamp,
    And the law a light;
    Reproofs of instruction are the way of life.

PROVERBS 6:20–23

Your word is a lamp to my feet
　　And a light to my path.
I have sworn and confirmed
　　That I will keep Your righteous judgments.
I am afflicted very much;
　　Revive me, O LORD, according to Your word.
Accept, I pray, the freewill offerings of my
　　　　　　mouth, O LORD,
　　And teach me Your judgments.

PSALM 119:105–108

The statutes of the LORD are right, rejoicing
　　　　　　the heart;
　　The commandment of the LORD is pure,
　　　　　　enlightening the eyes;
The fear of the LORD is clean, enduring forever;
　　The judgments of the LORD are true and
　　　　　　righteous altogether.
More to be desired are they than gold,
　　Yea, than much fine gold;
　　Sweeter also than honey and the honeycomb.
Moreover by them Your servant is warned,
　　And in keeping them there is great reward.

PSALM 19:8–11

How can a young man cleanse his way?
    By taking heed according to Your word.
With my whole heart I have sought You;
    Oh, let me not wander from Your
        commandments!
Your word I have hidden in my heart,
    That I might not sin against You.
Blessed are You, O Lord!
    Teach me Your statutes.

PSALM 119:9–12

Then Jesus said to those Jews who believed Him, "If you abide in My word, you are My disciples indeed. And you shall know the truth, and the truth shall make you free."

JOHN 8:31–32

The steps of a good man are ordered by
        the Lord,
    And He delights in his way.
Though he fall, he shall not be utterly cast down;
    For the Lord upholds him with His hand. . . .
He is ever merciful, and lends;
    And his descendants are blessed.

PSALM 37:23–24, 26

The Bible *Is* My . . .

POWER SOURCE

I will love You, O LORD, my strength.
The LORD is my rock and my fortress and
      my deliverer;
  My God, my strength, in whom I will trust;
  My shield and the horn of my salvation,
      my stronghold.
I will call upon the LORD, who is worthy to
      be praised;
  So shall I be saved from my enemies.

PSALM 18:1–3

For this reason we also, since the day we heard it, do not cease to pray for you, and to ask that you may be filled with the knowledge of His will in all wisdom and spiritual understanding; . . . strengthened with all might, according to His glorious power, for all patience and longsuffering with joy; giving thanks to the Father who has qualified us to be partakers of the inheritance of the saints in the light.

COLOSSIANS 1:9, 11–12

For this reason I bow my knees to the Father of our Lord Jesus Christ, from whom the whole family in heaven and earth is named, that He would grant you, according to the riches of His glory, to be strengthened with might through His Spirit in the inner man, that Christ may dwell in your hearts through faith; that you, being rooted and grounded in love, may be able to comprehend with all the saints what is the width and length and depth and height—to know the love of Christ which passes knowledge; that you may be filled with all the fullness of God.

Now to Him who is able to do exceedingly abundantly above all that we ask or think, according to the power that works in us, to Him be glory in the church by Christ Jesus to all generations, forever and ever. Amen.

EPHESIANS 3:14–21

For though He was crucified in weakness, yet He lives by the power of God. For we also are weak in Him, but we shall live with Him by the power of God toward you.

2 CORINTHIANS 13:4

Finally, my brethren, be strong in the Lord and in the power of His might. Put on the whole armor of God, that you may be able to stand against the wiles of the devil. For we do not wrestle against flesh and blood, but against principalities, against powers, against the rulers of the darkness of this age, against spiritual hosts of wickedness in the heavenly places. Therefore take up the whole armor of God, that you may be able to withstand in the evil day, and having done all, to stand.

Stand therefore, having girded your waist with truth, having put on the breastplate of righteousness, and having shod your feet with the preparation of the gospel of peace; above all, taking the shield of faith with which you will be able to quench all the fiery darts of the wicked one. And take the helmet of salvation, and the sword of the Spirit, which is the word of God; praying always with all prayer and supplication in the Spirit, being watchful to this end with all perseverance and supplication for all the saints.

EPHESIANS 6:10–18

For God has not given us a spirit of fear, but of power and of love and of a sound mind.

2 TIMOTHY 1:7

The Lord is my light and my salvation;
   Whom shall I fear?
   The Lord is the strength of my life;
   Of whom shall I be afraid?
When the wicked came against me
   To eat up my flesh,
   My enemies and foes,
   They stumbled and fell.

PSALM 27:1–2

The Bible *Is* My . . .

DEPENDABLE AUTHORITY

—❧————————————————————❧—

"For as the rain comes down, and the snow
       from heaven,
  And do not return there,
  But water the earth,
  And make it bring forth and bud,
  That it may give seed to the sower
  And bread to the eater,
So shall My word be that goes forth from
      My mouth;
  It shall not return to Me void,
  But it shall accomplish what I please,
  And it shall prosper in the thing for which
      I sent it."

ISAIAH 55:10–11

Knowing this first, that no prophecy of Scripture
is of any private interpretation, for prophecy never
came by the will of man, but holy men of God
spoke as they were moved by the Holy Spirit.

2 PETER 1:20–21

For the word of God is living and powerful, and sharper than any two-edged sword, piercing even to the division of soul and spirit, and of joints and marrow, and is a discerner of the thoughts and intents of the heart. And there is no creature hidden from His sight, but all things are naked and open to the eyes of Him to whom we must give account.

HEBREWS 4:12–13

Every word of God is pure;
   He is a shield to those who put their trust
      in Him.

PROVERBS 30:5

Forever, O LORD,
   Your word is settled in heaven.

PSALM 119:89

Then the LORD said to Moses, "Write these words, for according to the tenor of these words I have made a covenant with you and with Israel."

EXODUS 34:27

"Most assuredly, I say to you, if anyone keeps My word he shall never see death."

JOHN 8:51

"If you abide in Me, and My words abide in you, you will ask what you desire, and it shall be done for you."

JOHN 15:7

Hold fast the pattern of sound words which you have heard from me, in faith and love which are in Christ Jesus.

2 TIMOTHY 1:13

The counsel of the LORD stands forever,
   The plans of His heart to all generations.

PSALM 33:11

The Bible *Is* My . . .

WAY TO SUCCESS

———————————————————

"So now, brethren, I commend you to God and to the word of His grace, which is able to build you up and give you an inheritance among all those who are sanctified. . . . I have shown you in every way, by laboring like this, that you must support the weak. And remember the words of the Lord Jesus, that He said, 'It is more blessed to give than to receive.'"

ACTS 20:32, 35

For you did not receive the spirit of bondage again to fear, but you received the Spirit of adoption by whom we cry out, "Abba, Father." The Spirit Himself bears witness with our spirit that we are children of God, and if children, then heirs—heirs of God and joint heirs with Christ, if indeed we suffer with Him, that we may also be glorified together.

ROMANS 8:15–17

In Him also we have obtained an inheritance, being predestined according to the purpose of Him who works all things according to the counsel of His will, that we who first trusted in Christ should be to the praise of His glory.

In Him you also trusted, after you heard the word of truth, the gospel of your salvation; in whom also, having believed, you were sealed with the Holy Spirit of promise, who is the guarantee of our inheritance until the redemption of the purchased possession, to the praise of His glory.

EPHESIANS 1:11–14

And whatever you do, do it heartily, as to the Lord and not to men, knowing that from the Lord you will receive the reward of the inheritance; for you serve the Lord Christ.

COLOSSIANS 3:23–24

But thanks be to God, who gives us the victory through our Lord Jesus Christ.

1 CORINTHIANS 15:57

Command those who are rich in this present age not to be haughty, nor to trust in uncertain riches but in the living God, who gives us richly all things to enjoy. Let them do good, that they be rich in good works, ready to give, willing to share, storing up for themselves a good foundation for the time to come, that they may lay hold on eternal life.

1 TIMOTHY 6:17–19

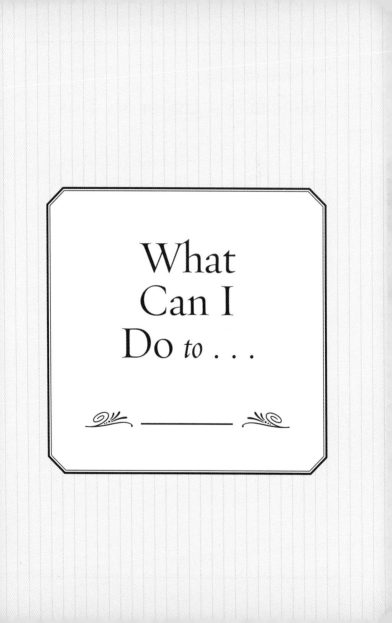

What Can I Do to . . .

What Can I Do *to* . . .

MAKE BETTER USE OF MY TIME?

❧————————————————❧

What profit has the worker from that in which he labors? I have seen the God-given task with which the sons of men are to be occupied. He has made everything beautiful in its time. Also He has put eternity in their hearts, except that no one can find out the work that God does from beginning to end.

I know that nothing is better for them than to rejoice, and to do good in their lives, and also that every man should eat and drink and enjoy the good of all his labor—it is the gift of God.

I know that whatever God does,
It shall be forever.
Nothing can be added to it,
And nothing taken from it.
God does it, that men should fear before Him.

ECCLESIASTES 3:9–14

Do not overwork to be rich;
    Because of your own understanding, cease!
Will you set your eyes on that which is not?
    For riches certainly make themselves wings;
    They fly away like an eagle toward heaven.
                                    PROVERBS 23:4–5

So teach us to number our days,
    That we may gain a heart of wisdom.
                                    PSALM 90:12

He who walks with wise men will be wise,
    But the companion of fools will be destroyed.
                                    PROVERBS 13:20

He who keeps his command will experience
        nothing harmful;
    And a wise man's heart discerns both time
        and judgment,
Because for every matter there is a time
        and judgment,
    Though the misery of man increases greatly.
For he does not know what will happen;
    So who can tell him when it will occur?
                                    ECCLESIASTES 8:5–7

He who has a slack hand becomes poor,
   But the hand of the diligent makes rich.
He who gathers in summer is a wise son;
   He who sleeps in harvest is a son who
      causes shame.
PROVERBS 10:4–5

Whoever loves instruction loves knowledge,
   But he who hates correction is stupid.
PROVERBS 12:1

The hand of the diligent will rule,
   But the lazy man will be put to forced labor.
PROVERBS 12:24

What Can I Do *to* . . .

Please God?

For this reason we also, since the day we heard it, do not cease to pray for you, and to ask that you may be filled with the knowledge of His will in all wisdom and spiritual understanding; that you may walk worthy of the Lord, fully pleasing Him, being fruitful in every good work and increasing in the knowledge of God; strengthened with all might, according to His glorious power, for all patience and longsuffering with joy; giving thanks to the Father who has qualified us to be partakers of the inheritance of the saints in the light.

Colossians 1:9–12

I beseech you therefore, brethren, by the mercies of God, that you present your bodies a living sacrifice, holy, acceptable to God, which is your reasonable service. And do not be conformed to this world, but be transformed by the renewing of your mind, that you may prove what is that good and acceptable and perfect will of God.

Romans 12:1–2

But without faith it is impossible to please Him, for he who comes to God must believe that He is, and that He is a rewarder of those who diligently seek Him.

HEBREWS 11:6

"Take heed that you do not do your charitable deeds before men, to be seen by them. Otherwise you have no reward from your Father in heaven."

MATTHEW 6:1

Therefore I exhort first of all that supplications, prayers, intercessions, and giving of thanks be made for all men, for kings and all who are in authority, that we may lead a quiet and peaceable life in all godliness and reverence. For this is good and acceptable in the sight of God our Savior, who desires all men to be saved and to come to the knowledge of the truth. . . .

I desire therefore that the men pray everywhere, lifting up holy hands, without wrath and doubting.

1 TIMOTHY 2:1–4, 8

Therefore by Him let us continually offer the sacrifice of praise to God, that is, the fruit of our lips, giving thanks to His name. But do not forget to do good and to share, for with such sacrifices God is well pleased.

HEBREWS 13:15–16

What Can I Do *to* . . .

GROW IN THE SPIRIT?

Therefore, laying aside all malice, all deceit, hypocrisy, envy, and all evil speaking, as new-born babes, desire the pure milk of the word, that you may grow thereby, if indeed you have tasted that the Lord is gracious.

1 PETER 2:1–3

Brethren, if a man is overtaken in any trespass, you who are spiritual restore such a one in a spirit of gentleness, considering yourself lest you also be tempted. Bear one another's burdens, and so fulfill the law of Christ. For if anyone thinks himself to be something, when he is nothing, he deceives himself. But let each one examine his own work, and then he will have rejoicing in himself alone, and not in another. For each one shall bear his own load.

GALATIANS 6:1–5

But also for this very reason, giving all diligence, add to your faith virtue, to virtue knowledge, to knowledge self-control, to self-control perseverance, to perseverance godliness, to godliness brotherly kindness, and to brotherly kindness love. For if these things are yours and abound, you will be neither barren nor unfruitful in the knowledge of our Lord Jesus Christ.

2 PETER 1:5–8

For this reason I bow my knees to the Father of our Lord Jesus Christ, from whom the whole family in heaven and earth is named, that He would grant you, according to the riches of His glory, to be strengthened with might through His Spirit in the inner man, that Christ may dwell in your hearts through faith; that you, being rooted and grounded in love, may be able to comprehend with all the saints what is the width and length and depth and height—to know the love of Christ which passes knowledge; that you may be filled with all the fullness of God.

EPHESIANS 3:14–19

Therefore, leaving the discussion of the elementary principles of Christ, let us go on to perfection, not laying again the foundation of repentance from dead works and of faith toward God, of the doctrine of baptisms, of laying on of hands, of resurrection of the dead, and of eternal judgment. And this we will do if God permits.

HEBREWS 6:1–3

But the fruit of the Spirit is love, joy, peace, long-suffering, kindness, goodness, faithfulness, gentleness, self-control. Against such there is no law.

GALATIANS 5:22–23

Being confident of this very thing, that He who has begun a good work in you will complete it until the day of Jesus Christ; . . .

And this I pray, that your love may abound still more and more in knowledge and all discernment, that you may approve the things that are excellent, that you may be sincere and without offense till the day of Christ.

PHILIPPIANS 1:6, 9–10

What Can I Do *to* . . .

INFLUENCE THE WORLD?

❧━━━━━━━━━━━━━━━━━━❧

"But rise and stand on your feet; for I have appeared to you for this purpose, to make you a minister and a witness both of the things which you have seen and of the things which I will yet reveal to you."

ACTS 26:16

"You are the light of the world. A city that is set on a hill cannot be hidden. Nor do they light a lamp and put it under a basket, but on a lampstand, and it gives light to all who are in the house. Let your light so shine before men, that they may see your good works and glorify your Father in heaven."

MATTHEW 5:14–16

"Most assuredly, I say to you, he who believes in Me, the works that I do he will do also; and greater works than these he will do, because I go to My Father."

JOHN 14:12

And He said to them, "Go into all the world and preach the gospel to every creature. He who believes and is baptized will be saved; but he who does not believe will be condemned. And these signs will follow those who believe: In My name they will cast out demons; they will speak with new tongues; they will take up serpents; and if they drink anything deadly, it will by no means hurt them; they will lay hands on the sick, and they will recover."

So then, after the Lord had spoken to them, He was received up into heaven, and sat down at the right hand of God. And they went out and preached everywhere, the Lord working with them and confirming the word through the accompanying signs. Amen.

MARK 16:15–20

"The Spirit of the LORD is upon Me,
Because He has anointed Me
To preach the gospel to the poor;
He has sent Me to heal the brokenhearted,
To proclaim liberty to the captives
And recovery of sight to the blind,
To set at liberty those who are oppressed;
To proclaim the acceptable year of the LORD."

LUKE 4:18–19

For this is the love of God, that we keep His commandments. And His commandments are not burdensome. For whatever is born of God overcomes the world. And this is the victory that has overcome the world—our faith. Who is he who overcomes the world, but he who believes that Jesus is the Son of God?

1 JOHN 5:3–5

How then shall they call on Him in whom they have not believed? And how shall they believe in Him of whom they have not heard? And how shall they hear without a preacher? And how shall they preach unless they are sent? As it is written:

"How beautiful are the feet of those who
    preach the gospel of peace,
Who bring glad tidings of good things!"

ROMANS 10:14–15

What Can I Do *to* . . .

COUNT MY BLESSINGS?

For the Scripture says, "Whoever believes on Him will not be put to shame." For there is no distinction between Jew and Greek, for the same Lord over all is rich to all who call upon Him. For "whoever calls on the name of the LORD shall be saved."

ROMANS 10:11–13

For the law was given through Moses, but grace and truth came through Jesus Christ.

JOHN 1:17

Every good gift and every perfect gift is from above, and comes down from the Father of lights, with whom there is no variation or shadow of turning. Of His own will He brought us forth by the word of truth, that we might be a kind of firstfruits of His creatures.

JAMES 1:17–18

Blessed be the God and Father of our Lord Jesus Christ, who has blessed us with every spiritual blessing in the heavenly places in Christ, just as He chose us in Him before the foundation of the world, that we should be holy and without blame before Him in love.

EPHESIANS 1:3–4

Thanks be to God for His indescribable gift!

2 CORINTHIANS 9:15

Both riches and honor come from You,
    And You reign over all.
    In Your hand is power and might;
    In Your hand it is to make great
    And to give strength to all.
Now therefore, our God,
    We thank You
    And praise Your glorious name.

1 CHRONICLES 29:12–13

And above all things have fervent love for one another, for "love will cover a multitude of sins."

1 PETER 4:8

Open to me the gates of righteousness;
    I will go through them,
    And I will praise the LORD.
This is the gate of the LORD,
    Through which the righteous shall enter.
I will praise You,
    For You have answered me,
    And have become my salvation.

PSALM 118:19–21

Making a
Difference

by . . .

Making a Difference *by* . . .

USING MY GIFTS FOR GOD

❧━━━━━━━━━━━━━━━━━━━━━━━━━❧

As each one has received a gift, minister it to one another, as good stewards of the manifold grace of God. If anyone speaks, let him speak as the oracles of God. If anyone ministers, let him do it as with the ability which God supplies, that in all things God may be glorified through Jesus Christ, to whom belong the glory and the dominion forever and ever. Amen.

1 PETER 4:10–11

And whatever you do, do it heartily, as to the Lord and not to men, knowing that from the Lord you will receive the reward of the inheritance; for you serve the Lord Christ.

COLOSSIANS 3:23–24

Therefore I remind you to stir up the gift of God which is in you through the laying on of my hands. For God has not given us a spirit of fear, but of power and of love and of a sound mind.

2 TIMOTHY 1:6–7

Do not neglect the gift that is in you, which was given to you by prophecy with the laying on of the hands of the eldership. Meditate on these things; give yourself entirely to them, that your progress may be evident to all. Take heed to yourself and to the doctrine. Continue in them, for in doing this you will save both yourself and those who hear you.

1 Timothy 4:14–16

Even so you, since you are zealous for spiritual gifts, let it be for the edification of the church that you seek to excel.

1 Corinthians 14:12

So let each one give as he purposes in his heart, not grudgingly or of necessity; for God loves a cheerful giver.

2 Corinthians 9:7

Making a Difference *by* . . .

MAKING EVERY DAY COUNT

━━━━━━━━━━━━━━━━━━━━━━━━

LORD, make me to know my end,
    And what is the measure of my days,
    That I may know how frail I am.
Indeed, You have made my days as handbreadths,
    And my age is as nothing before You;
    Certainly every man at his best state is
        but vapor.
Surely every man walks about like a shadow;
    Surely they busy themselves in vain;
    He heaps up riches,
    And does not know who will gather them.
And now, Lord, what do I wait for?
    My hope is in You.

PSALM 39:4–7

Be diligent to present yourself approved to God, a
worker who does not need to be ashamed, rightly
dividing the word of truth.

2 TIMOTHY 2:15

He who tills his land will be satisfied with bread,
    But he who follows frivolity is devoid
        of understanding. . . .
A man will be satisfied with good by the
        fruit of his mouth,
    And the recompense of a man's hands will
        be rendered to him. . . .
The hand of the diligent will rule,
    But the lazy man will be put to forced labor.

PROVERBS 12:11, 14, 24

One person esteems one day above another; another esteems every day alike. Let each be fully convinced in his own mind. He who observes the day, observes it to the Lord; and he who does not observe the day, to the Lord he does not observe it.

ROMANS 14:5–6

Be sober, be vigilant; because your adversary the devil walks about like a roaring lion, seeking whom he may devour.

1 PETER 5:8

Making a Difference *by* . . .

SHARING MY FAITH

—⚜———————————⚜—

Fight the good fight of faith, lay hold on eternal life, to which you were also called and have confessed the good confession in the presence of many witnesses. I urge you in the sight of God who gives life to all things, and before Christ Jesus who witnessed the good confession before Pontius Pilate, that you keep this commandment without spot, blameless until our Lord Jesus Christ's appearing, which He will manifest in His own time, He who is the blessed and only Potentate, the King of kings and Lord of lords, who alone has immortality, dwelling in unapproachable light, whom no man has seen or can see, to whom be honor and everlasting power. Amen.

1 TIMOTHY 6:12–16

A faithful witness does not lie,
But a false witness will utter lies.

PROVERBS 14:5

"Go therefore and make disciples of all the nations, baptizing them in the name of the Father and of the Son and of the Holy Spirit, teaching them to observe all things that I have commanded you; and lo, I am with you always, even to the end of the age." Amen.

MATTHEW 28:19–20

Let us draw near with a true heart in full assurance of faith, having our hearts sprinkled from an evil conscience and our bodies washed with pure water. Let us hold fast the confession of our hope without wavering, for He who promised is faithful. And let us consider one another in order to stir up love and good works, not forsaking the assembling of ourselves together, as is the manner of some, but exhorting one another, and so much the more as you see the Day approaching.

HEBREWS 10:22–25

Whoever walks blamelessly will be saved,
But he who is perverse in his ways will
suddenly fall. . . .
A faithful man will abound with blessings,
But he who hastens to be rich will not
go unpunished.

PROVERBS 28:18, 20

Therefore do not be ashamed of the testimony of our Lord, nor of me His prisoner, but share with me in the sufferings for the gospel according to the power of God, who has saved us and called us with a holy calling, not according to our works, but according to His own purpose and grace which was given to us in Christ Jesus before time began.

2 TIMOTHY 1:8–9

Making a Difference *by* . . .

LISTENING TO HIS VOICE

❧━━━━━━━━━━━━━━━━❧

"Ho! Everyone who thirsts,
    Come to the waters;
    And you who have no money,
    Come, buy and eat.
    Yes, come, buy wine and milk
    Without money and without price.
Why do you spend money for what is not
            bread,
    And your wages for what does not satisfy?
    Listen carefully to Me, and eat what is good,
    And let your soul delight itself in abundance.
Incline your ear, and come to Me.
    Hear, and your soul shall live;
    And I will make an everlasting covenant
            with you—
    The sure mercies of David."

ISAIAH 55:1–3

But whoever listens to me will dwell safely,
    And will be secure, without fear of evil.

PROVERBS 1:33

He who answers a matter before he hears it,
It is folly and shame to him. . . .
The heart of the prudent acquires knowledge,
And the ear of the wise seeks knowledge.

PROVERBS 18:13, 15

Cease listening to instruction, my son,
And you will stray from the words
of knowledge.

PROVERBS 19:27

So then, my beloved brethren, let every man be swift to hear, slow to speak, slow to wrath.

JAMES 1:19

God's
Answers
About My
Lifestyle . . .

God's Answers *About* My Lifestyle . . .

SERVING GOD AND OTHERS

"You are My friends if you do whatever I command you. No longer do I call you servants, for a servant does not know what his master is doing; but I have called you friends, for all things that I heard from My Father I have made known to you. You did not choose Me, but I chose you and appointed you that you should go and bear fruit, and that your fruit should remain, that whatever you ask the Father in My name He may give you."

JOHN 15:14–16

Bondservants, be obedient to those who are your masters according to the flesh, with fear and trembling, in sincerity of heart, as to Christ; not with eyeservice, as men-pleasers, but as bondservants of Christ, doing the will of God from the heart, with goodwill doing service, as to the Lord, and not to men, knowing that whatever good anyone does, he will receive the same from the Lord, whether he is a slave or free.

EPHESIANS 6:5–8

"He who loves his life will lose it, and he who hates his life in this world will keep it for eternal life. If anyone serves Me, let him follow Me; and where I am, there My servant will be also. If anyone serves Me, him My Father will honor."

JOHN 12:25–26

"Therefore, when you do a charitable deed, do not sound a trumpet before you as the hypocrites do in the synagogues and in the streets, that they may have glory from men. Assuredly, I say to you, they have their reward. But when you do a charitable deed, do not let your left hand know what your right hand is doing, that your charitable deed may be in secret; and your Father who sees in secret will Himself reward you openly."

MATTHEW 6:2–4

Do as those who will be judged by the law of liberty. For judgment is without mercy to the one who has shown no mercy. Mercy triumphs over judgment.

What does it profit, my brethren, if someone says he has faith but does not have works? Can faith save him?

JAMES 2:12–14

Serve the LORD with gladness;
 Come before His presence with singing.
Know that the LORD, He is God;
 It is He who has made us, and not
  we ourselves;
 We are His people and the sheep of
  His pasture.
Enter into His gates with thanksgiving,
 And into His courts with praise.
 Be thankful to Him, and bless His name.
For the LORD is good;
 His mercy is everlasting,
 And His truth endures to all generations.

PSALM 100:2–5

If there is among you a poor man of your brethren, within any of the gates in your land which the LORD your God is giving you, you shall not harden your heart nor shut your hand from your poor brother, but you shall open your hand wide to him and willingly lend him sufficient for his need, whatever he needs.

DEUTERONOMY 15:7–8

God's Answers *About* My Lifestyle . . .

WHEN LIFE IS HARD

"Behold, I am coming quickly! Hold fast what you have, that no one may take your crown. He who overcomes, I will make him a pillar in the temple of My God, and he shall go out no more. I will write on him the name of My God and the name of the city of My God, the New Jerusalem, which comes down out of heaven from My God. And I will write on him My new name."

REVELATION 3:11–12

My brethren, count it all joy when you fall into various trials, knowing that the testing of your faith produces patience. But let patience have its perfect work, that you may be perfect and complete, lacking nothing. If any of you lacks wisdom, let him ask of God, who gives to all liberally and without reproach, and it will be given to him. But let him ask in faith, with no doubting, for he who doubts is like a wave of the sea driven and tossed by the wind.

JAMES 1:2–6

Beloved, do not think it strange concerning the fiery trial which is to try you, as though some strange thing happened to you; but rejoice to the extent that you partake of Christ's sufferings, that when His glory is revealed, you may also be glad with exceeding joy. If you are reproached for the name of Christ, blessed are you, for the Spirit of glory and of God rests upon you.

1 PETER 4:12–14

And now, little children, abide in Him, that when He appears, we may have confidence and not be ashamed before Him at His coming.

1 JOHN 2:28

Beware, brethren, lest there be in any of you an evil heart of unbelief in departing from the living God; but exhort one another daily, while it is called "Today," lest any of you be hardened through the deceitfulness of sin. For we have become partakers of Christ if we hold the beginning of our confidence steadfast to the end, while it is said:

"Today, if you will hear His voice,
Do not harden your hearts as in the rebellion."

HEBREWS 3:12–15

Oh come, let us sing to the LORD!
    Let us shout joyfully to the Rock of
        our salvation.
Let us come before His presence with
        thanksgiving;
    Let us shout joyfully to Him with psalms.
For the LORD is the great God,
    And the great King above all gods.
In His hand are the deep places of the earth;
    The heights of the hills are His also.
The sea is His, for He made it;
    And His hands formed the dry land.
Oh come, let us worship and bow down;
    Let us kneel before the LORD our Maker.
For He is our God,
    And we are the people of His pasture,
    And the sheep of His hand.

PSALM 95:1–7

God's Answers *About* My Lifestyle . . .

WHEN NOTHING IS GOING RIGHT

Trust in the LORD with all your heart,
 And lean not on your own understanding;
In all your ways acknowledge Him,
 And He shall direct your paths.

PROVERBS 3:5–6

For you were once darkness, but now you are light in the Lord. Walk as children of light (for the fruit of the Spirit is in all goodness, righteousness, and truth), finding out what is acceptable to the Lord. And have no fellowship with the unfruitful works of darkness, but rather expose them. For it is shameful even to speak of those things which are done by them in secret. But all things that are exposed are made manifest by the light, for whatever makes manifest is light. Therefore He says:

"Awake, you who sleep,
 Arise from the dead,
 And Christ will give you light."

EPHESIANS 5:8–14

I wait for the LORD, my soul waits,
    And in His word I do hope.
My soul waits for the Lord
    More than those who watch for the morning—
    Yes, more than those who watch for
        the morning.

PSALM 130:5–6

Come now, you who say, "Today or tomorrow we will go to such and such a city, spend a year there, buy and sell, and make a profit"; whereas you do not know what will happen tomorrow. For what is your life? It is even a vapor that appears for a little time and then vanishes away. Instead you ought to say, "If the Lord wills, we shall live and do this or that."

JAMES 4:13–15

"For I know the thoughts that I think toward you, says the LORD, thoughts of peace and not of evil, to give you a future and a hope. Then you will call upon Me and go and pray to Me, and I will listen to you. And you will seek Me and find Me, when you search for Me with all your heart."

JEREMIAH 29:11–13

Our soul waits for the LORD;
   He is our help and our shield.
For our heart shall rejoice in Him,
   Because we have trusted in His holy name.
Let Your mercy, O LORD, be upon us,
   Just as we hope in You.

PSALM 33:20–22

There are many plans in a man's heart,
   Nevertheless the LORD's counsel—that
      will stand.

PROVERBS 19:21

God's Answers *About* My Lifestyle . . .

WHEN I FEEL DESERTED

❧ ———————————— ❧

Be strong and of good courage, do not fear nor be afraid of them; for the LORD your God, He is the One who goes with you. He will not leave you nor forsake you.

DEUTERONOMY 31:6

"Because he has set his love upon Me,
    therefore I will deliver him;
  I will set him on high, because he has known
    My name.
He shall call upon Me, and I will answer him;
  I will be with him in trouble;
  I will deliver him and honor him.
With long life I will satisfy him,
  And show him My salvation."

PSALM 91:14–16

You will keep him in perfect peace,
  Whose mind is stayed on You,
  Because he trusts in You.

ISAIAH 26:3

Hear, O LORD, when I cry with my voice!
    Have mercy also upon me, and answer me.
When You said, "Seek My face,"
    My heart said to You, "Your face, LORD,
        I will seek."
Do not hide Your face from me;
    Do not turn Your servant away in anger;
    You have been my help;
    Do not leave me nor forsake me,
    O God of my salvation.
When my father and my mother forsake me,
    Then the LORD will take care of me.

PSALM 27:7–10

How precious is Your lovingkindness, O God!
    Therefore the children of men put their trust
        under the shadow of Your wings.
They are abundantly satisfied with the fullness
        of Your house,
    And You give them drink from the river of
        Your pleasures.
For with You is the fountain of life;
    In Your light we see light.

PSALM 36:7–9

"Indeed the hour is coming, yes, has now come, that you will be scattered, each to his own, and will leave Me alone. And yet I am not alone, because the Father is with Me."

JOHN 16:32

Teach me, O LORD, the way of Your statutes,
    And I shall keep it to the end.
Give me understanding, and I shall keep
        Your law;
    Indeed, I shall observe it with my whole heart.
Make me walk in the path of Your
        commandments,
    For I delight in it.
Incline my heart to Your testimonies,
    And not to covetousness.
Turn away my eyes from looking at
        worthless things,
    And revive me in Your way.
Establish Your word to Your servant,
    Who is devoted to fearing You.
Turn away my reproach which I dread,
    For Your judgments are good.
Behold, I long for Your precepts;
    Revive me in Your righteousness.

PSALM 119:33–40

God's Answers *About* My Lifestyle . . .

WHEN I DON'T UNDERSTAND HIS WAYS

As for God, His way is perfect;
   The word of the LORD is proven;
   He is a shield to all who trust in Him.
For who is God, except the LORD?
   And who is a rock, except our God?
It is God who arms me with strength,
   And makes my way perfect.
He makes my feet like the feet of deer,
   And sets me on my high places.

PSALM 18:30–33

Let us hold fast the confession of our hope without wavering, for He who promised is faithful. And let us consider one another in order to stir up love and good works, not forsaking the assembling of ourselves together, as is the manner of some, but exhorting one another, and so much the more as you see the Day approaching.

HEBREWS 10:23–25

"For My thoughts are not your thoughts,
Nor are your ways My ways," says the LORD.
"For as the heavens are higher than the earth,
So are My ways higher than your ways,
And My thoughts than your thoughts.
For as the rain comes down, and the snow
from heaven,
And do not return there,
But water the earth,
And make it bring forth and bud,
That it may give seed to the sower
And bread to the eater,
So shall My word be that goes forth from
My mouth;
It shall not return to Me void,
But it shall accomplish what I please,
And it shall prosper in the thing for which
I sent it.
For you shall go out with joy,
And be led out with peace;
The mountains and the hills
Shall break forth into singing before you,
And all the trees of the field shall clap
their hands."

ISAIAH 55:8–12

"And I will make an everlasting covenant with them, that I will not turn away from doing them good; but I will put My fear in their hearts so that they will not depart from Me. Yes, I will rejoice over them to do them good, and I will assuredly plant them in this land, with all My heart and with all My soul."

JEREMIAH 32:40–41

Be merciful to me, O God, be merciful to me!
    For my soul trusts in You;
    And in the shadow of Your wings I will make
        my refuge,
    Until these calamities have passed by.

I will cry out to God Most High,
    To God who performs all things for me.
He shall send from heaven and save me;
    He reproaches the one who would swallow
        me up.
    God shall send forth His mercy and His truth.

PSALM 57:1–3

And we know that all things work together for good to those who love God, to those who are the called according to His purpose.

ROMANS 8:28